Latin
FOR COMMON ENTRANCE

13+ LEVEL 3

Exam Practice Answers

R.C. Bass

GALORE PARK

AN HACHETTE UK COMPANY

About the author

Bob Bass taught at prep schools in Somerset, Kenya and Sussex before moving in 1987 to Orwell Park, Ipswich, where he is Head of Classics and Senior Master. He has served on the editorial board of the *Journal of Classics Teaching* and on the Council of the Joint Association of Classical Teachers. For 12 years he edited the SATIPS Classics Broadsheet, and has been IAPS' Subject Leader and then Subject Adviser in Classics. He is the Chief Setter of ISEB's Common Entrance and Common Academic Scholarship Latin papers, proofreader for their Greek papers, and an IGCSE examiner. He is the author of various Latin and Greek resources targeted at young learners.

Every effort has been made to trace all copyright holders, but if any have been inadvertently overlooked, the Publishers will be pleased to make the necessary arrangements at the first opportunity.

Although every effort has been made to ensure that website addresses are correct at time of going to press, Galore Park cannot be held responsible for the content of any website mentioned in this book. It is sometimes possible to find a relocated web page by typing in the address of the home page for a website in the URL window of your browser.

Hachette UK's policy is to use papers that are natural, renewable and recyclable products and made from wood grown in sustainable forests. The logging and manufacturing processes are expected to conform to the environmental regulations of the country of origin.

Orders: please contact Bookpoint Ltd, 130 Milton Park, Abingdon, Oxon OX14 4SB. Telephone: (44) 01235 827720. Fax: (44) 01235 400454. Email education@bookpoint.co.uk Lines are open from 9 a.m. to 5 p.m., Monday to Saturday, with a 24-hour message answering service. Visit our website at www.galorepark.co.uk for details of other revision guides for Common Entrance, examination papers and Galore Park publications.

ISBN: 978 1 471853 50 0

© Robert C. Bass 2015

First published in 2015 by
Galore Park Publishing Ltd,
An Hachette UK Company
Carmelite House
50 Victoria Embankment
London EC4Y 0DZ
www.galorepark.co.uk

Impression number   10 9 8 7 6 5 4 3 2 1

Year   2019 2018 2017 2016 2015

Typeset in India

Printed in the United Kingdom

A catalogue record for this title is available from the British Library.

Contents

Introduction

A note on translation into English

The present tense in Latin may be translated using either of two aspects: the present simple (**amo** = I love) or the present continuous/progressive (**amo** = I am loving).

The imperfect tense may be translated as either **amabam** = I was loving or **amabam** = I used to love.

The perfect tense may be translated as a simple past (**amavi** = I loved) or as a 'true' perfect (**amavi** = I have loved).

Note also that, as Latin has neither a definite article nor an indefinite article, the use of 'the' and 'a/an' can often be interchangeable; sometimes neither is required.

Equally, the 3rd person singular may be translated by 'he', 'she' or 'it' and pupils should not be penalised where their choice does not match the answer given in this book. However, with the perfect passive, the gender is established by the ending of the participle, e.g. **pulsus est** = he was driven, **pulsa est** = she was driven and **pulsum est** = it was driven.

The syllabus and your exams

For Common Entrance Latin, you will sit an exam lasting one hour. You will choose one of the three levels, Level 1, Level 2 or Level 3, as agreed with your teacher.

The format of each level is the same, but the material gets harder. In each level, there are four questions worth a total of 75 marks, as follows:

Question 1 (15 marks)

A short passage of Latin will be set, on which you will be asked to answer eight to ten questions, testing your understanding of the passage. You will not be expected to write a translation of the passage, but clearly you need to have translated it in your head, in order to answer the questions.

Question 2 (30 marks)

Another, slightly longer passage will be set, continuing the story from the passage in Question 1. You will be asked to translate this passage, writing your translation on alternate lines.

Question 3 (20 marks)

Another short passage of Latin will be set, continuing the story from the earlier two passages. Questions will be set, testing your knowledge of Latin grammar and how the language works. You will not be asked to translate this passage, but again you will find it difficult to answer the questions unless you have translated it for yourself.

The questions will fall into the following types:

● From the passage give, in Latin, one example of: (an adjective, a preposition followed by the accusative, a noun in the genitive, a verb in the imperfect tense, etc.)

● **erat** (line 2). In which tense is this verb? What is the 1st person singular of the present tense of this verb?

● **pueros** (line 4). In which case is this noun? Why is this case used?

● **vocaverunt** (line 5). What does this word mean? What is the connection between vocaverunt and the English word *vocation*?

- **necat** (line 5) means *he kills*. How would you say in Latin *he was killing* (imperfect tense)?

And last but not least:

- Using the vocabulary given, translate the following two short sentences into Latin.

Most candidates lose the majority of their marks on Question 3 by falling into the trap of thinking they do not need to translate the passage. They simply guess the answers. To answer a question such as 'in which case is the word **templum** in line 3?', you have to have translated the sentence in which the word **templum** is. Otherwise you will simply be guessing, particularly with a word such as **templum**, which could be any of nominative, vocative or accusative singular.

Question 4 (10 marks)

You will be set eight questions on four areas: Roman domestic life; the city of Rome; the army and Roman Britain; and Greek mythology. Each question will have two parts, part (i) and part (ii). You select **one** question, and answer both parts of it. Examples are given below:

The city of Rome

(c) (i) Tell the story of Cloelia.

    (ii) Which elements of this story would the Romans have found particularly admirable? Explain your answer.

Greek mythology

(h) (i) Tell the story of Odysseus' encounter with the Cyclops.

    (ii) Describe two qualities which Odysseus displayed in this encounter.

These are two of the eight questions that might have been set, labelled (a) to (h). If you had chosen to do the one labelled (c) above, you would have done both part (i) and part (ii) of that question.

Tips on revising

Get the best out of your brain

- Give your brain plenty of oxygen by exercising. You can only revise effectively if you feel fit and well.
- Eat healthy food while you are revising. Your brain works better when you give it good fuel.
- Think positively. Give your brain positive messages so that it will want to study.
- Keep calm. If your brain is stressed, it will not operate effectively.
- Take regular breaks during your study time.
- Get enough sleep. Your brain will carry on sorting out what you have revised while you sleep.

Get the most from your revision

- Don't work for hours without a break. Revise for 20–30 minutes, then take a five-minute break.
- Do good things in your breaks: listen to your favourite music, eat healthy food, drink some water, do some exercise or juggle. Don't read a book, watch TV or play on the computer; it will conflict with what your brain is trying to learn.
- When you go back to your revision, review what you have just learnt.
- Regularly review the material you have learnt.

Get motivated

- Set yourself some goals and promise yourself a treat when the exams are over.
- Make the most of all the expertise and talent available to you at school and at home. If you don't understand something, ask your teacher to explain.
- Get organised. Find a quiet place to revise and make sure you have all the equipment you need.
- Use year and weekly planners to help you organise your time so that you revise all subjects equally. (Available for download from www.galorepark.co.uk)
- Use topic and subject checklists to help you keep on top of what you are revising. (Available for download from www.galorepark.co.uk)

Know what to expect in the exam

- Use past papers to familiarise yourself with the format of the exam.
- Make sure you understand the language examiners use.

Before the exam

- Have all your equipment and pens ready the night before.
- Make sure you are at your best by getting a good night's sleep before the exam.
- Have a good breakfast in the morning.
- Take some water into the exam if you are allowed.
- Think positively and keep calm.

During the exam

- Have a watch on your desk. Work out how much time you need to allocate to each question and try to stick to it.
- Make sure you read and understand the instructions on the front of the exam paper.
- Allow some time at the start to read and consider the questions carefully before writing anything.
- Read every question at least twice. Don't rush into answering before you have a chance to think about it.

Exercise 1.1

The Greeks were destroying the city of Troy.(4) They were killing many Trojan soldiers.(4) They were burning many temples.(3) They were capturing many citizens.(3) Aeneas was a Trojan chieftain.(4) When he saw Greek soldiers standing in the middle of the city,(6) he called his friends together(2) and said these words to them:(5)

'Friends, our city is being captured by the Greeks.(5) We are in very great danger.(3) Our soldiers are being killed.(3) Our temples are being burned.(3) Our citizens are being captured.(3) We ought to escape.(2) Take your weapons!(2) Abandon your homes!(2) Prepare the ships!(2) Let's leave immediately!'(2)

Weapons therefore are taken by the Trojans.(4) Homes are abandoned.(2) Ships are prepared.(2) Aeneas and his friends meet near the ships(5) and quickly depart from the city of Troy.(4)

Total: 75

Exercise 1.2

1 (a) delebant/necabant/incendebant/capiebant/erat. (1)

 (b) vidit/convocavit/dixit. (1)

 (c) maximo. (1)

2 3rd.   Singular.   dico. (3)

3 Vocative. (1)

4 Accusative.   Object of the verb. (2)

5 celeriter means 'quickly' and *accelerate* means to go faster or more quickly. (1)

Total: 10

Exercise 1.3

1 We are loved.

2 He is praised.

3 They are wounded.

4 You (s.) are called.

5 I am carried.

6 We are set free.

7 It is announced.

8 You (pl.) are praised.

9 They are killed.

10 You (pl.) are watched.

1 mark for each question. Total: 10

Exercise 1.4

1 He is warned.
2 You (pl.) are seen.
3 You (s.) are moved.
4 He is held.
5 You (s.) are frightened.

6 They are destroyed.
7 They are seen.
8 We are moved.
9 You (pl.) are warned.
10 We are ordered.

1 mark for each question. Total: 10

Exercise 1.5

1 We are ruled.
2 It is put.
3 You (pl.) are taken.
4 It is defended.
5 They are made.

6 You (s.) are sent.
7 They are handed over.
8 You (pl.) are killed.
9 They are conquered.
10 It is thrown.

1 mark for each question. Total: 10

Exercise 1.6

1 He is heard.
2 They are found.
3 I am punished.
4 You (pl.) are heard.
5 You (s.) are punished.

6 It is found.
7 We are punished.
8 You (s.) are heard.
9 They are heard.
10 He is punished.

1 mark for each question. Total: 10

Exercise 1.7

1 We are defended.
2 They are led.
3 It is destroyed.
4 We are watched.
5 It is read.

6 We are sent.
7 He is killed.
8 You (pl.) are put.
9 They are attacked.
10 They are punished.

1 mark for each question. Total: 10

Exercise 1.8

1 The enemy wounds the soldier.
2 The soldier is wounded by the enemy.

3 The young man reads the book.
4 The book is read by the young man.

5 The slaves prepare food.

6 Food is prepared by the slaves.

7 The teacher praises the boys.

8 The boys are praised by the teacher.

9 The enemy attack the city.

10 The city is attacked by the enemy.

3 marks for each question. Total: 30

Exercise 1.9

1 I love the girl.

2 The girl is loved by me.

3 The slaves drink the wine.

4 The wine is drunk by the slaves.

5 The Romans capture the town.

6 The town is captured by the Romans.

7 The king rules the land.

8 The land is ruled by the king.

9 The Greeks conquer the Romans.

10 The Romans are conquered by the Greeks.

3 marks for each question. Total: 30

Exercise 1.10

1 The Romans always conquer the Greeks. (4)

2 The Greeks are always conquered by the Romans. (5)

3 The master often punishes the slaves. (4)

4 The slaves are often punished by the master. (5)

5 The poet is always reading books. (4)

6 Books are always being read by the poet. (5)

7 You (s.) love your father. (2)

8 Father is loved by you. (4)

9 The soldiers are defending the city. (3)

10 The city is defended by the soldiers. (4)

Total: 40

Exercise 1.11

1 A storm destroys the ships. (3)

2 The ships are destroyed by a storm. (3)

3 The enemy do not like us. (4)

4 We are not liked by the enemy. (4)

5 The pupils like the teacher. (3)

6 The teacher is liked by the pupils. (4)

7 The citizens wound the king. (3)

8 The king is wounded by the citizens. (4)

9 The boy sees the city. (3)

10 The city is seen by the boy. (4)

Total: 35

Exercise 1.12

1 We are being watched by the enemy.

2 The enemy are killed with swords.

3 I am sent by the master.

4 I am loved by my father.

5 You (s.) are praised by the teacher.

6 The soldiers are wounded by arrows.

7 He is carried by a slave.

8 They are set free by the master.

9 You (pl.) are taken by the soldiers.

10 We are defended by the king.

3 marks for each question. Total: 30

Exercise 1.13

1 We are conquered by the Romans.

2 Marcus, I am wounded by spears.

3 I am watched by the boy.

4 We are ordered by the master.

5 The soldier is wounded by a sword.

6 We are praised by the teacher.

7 They are ruled by the queen.

8 You (pl.) are defended by the soldiers.

9 I am punished by the master.

10 We are led by the slaves.

3 marks for each question. Total: 30

Exercise 1.14

1 Sparta, a Greek city, is ruled by Menelaus. (6)

2 Helen, the wife of Menelaus, is a very beautiful woman. (6)

3 Helen however is taken by Paris. (5)

4 Helen is led to the city of Troy by Paris. (7)

5 Menelaus is angry. (3)

6 Many soldiers are called by Menelaus. (5)

7 Many ships are prepared by the Greeks. (5)

8 Soldiers are quickly put onto the ships. (5)

9 Soon the ships are sent across the sea to the city of Troy. (8)

10 Troy is attacked for a long time by the Greeks. (5)

Total: 55

Exercise 1.15

1 Many very brave men are killed in the war. (6)

2 Patroclus is killed by Hector. (4)

3 Hector is killed by Achilles. (4)

4 The body of Hector is seen by the Trojan citizens. (6)

5 The walls of Troy are not destroyed. (4)

6 The city is not captured by the Greeks. (5)

7 Finally a very big horse is built by the Greeks. (6)

8 The horse is put near the city of Troy. (5)

9 A soldier is left by the Greeks. (4)

10 The city of Troy is finally captured by the Greeks. (6)

Total: 50

Exercise 1.16

1 amamur.

2 moneris.

3 reguntur.

4 audior.

5 vincimini.

6 defendimur.

7 vulnerantur.

8 liberatur.

9 iubemur.

10 puniuntur.

1 mark for each question. Total: 10

Exercise 1.17

1 servi liberantur.

2 discipulus monetur.

3 urbs defenditur.

4 muri delentur.

5 pecunia invenitur.

2 marks for each question. Total: 10

Exercise 1.18

1 servus a domino liberatur. (4)

2 discipuli a magistro puniuntur. (4)

3 navis a militibus oppugnatur. (4)

4 patres a filiis saepe amantur. (5)

5 bella a feminis/mulieribus non amantur. (5)

6 multa oppida a Romanis oppugnantur. (5)

7 ille magister a discipulis numquam amatur. (6)

8 libri a pueris sapientibus saepe leguntur. (6)

9 Helena a Graecis reducitur. (4)

10 discipuli boni a magistris bonis semper laudantur. (7)

Total: 50

Exercise 1.19

1 You (pl.) take.	capimini.	You (pl.) are taken.
2 He hears.	auditur.	He is heard.
3 I see.	videor.	I am seen.
4 We wound.	vulneramur.	We are wounded.
5 You (s.) defend.	defenderis.	You (s.) are defended.
6 We warn.	monemur.	We are warned.
7 You (pl.) attack.	oppugnamini.	You (pl.) are attacked.
8 He punishes.	punitur.	He is punished.
9 You (s.) order.	iuberis.	You (s.) are ordered.
10 He catches sight of.	conspicitur.	He is caught sight of.

3 marks for each question. Total: 30

Exercise 1.20

1 You (pl.) are heard.	auditis.	You (pl.) hear.
2 We are attacked.	oppugnamus.	We attack.
3 They are led.	ducunt.	They lead.
4 They are abandoned.	relinquunt.	They abandon.
5 You (s.) are saved.	servas.	You (s.) save.
6 He is conquered.	vincit.	He conquers.
7 He is wounded.	vulnerat.	He wounds.
8 We are killed.	occidimus.	We kill.
9 They are set free.	liberant.	They set free.
10 I am ordered.	iubeo.	I order.

3 marks for each question. Total: 30

Exercise 1.21

1 monet.	He warns.
2 monetur.	He is warned.
3 convenimus.	We met.
4 reducebas.	You (s.) were leading back.
5 laudant.	They praise.
6 laudantur.	They are praised.
7 eritis.	You (pl.) will be.

8 potueram. I had been able.

9 ierunt/iverunt. They went.

10 vulneraris. You (pl.) are wounded.

2 marks for each question. Total: 20

Exercise 1.22

1 They will meet.	3rd person	Plural	Future	Active	**convenio**
2 They ran.	3rd person	Plural	Perfect	Active	**curro**
3 He gave.	3rd person	Singular	Perfect	Active	**do**
4 They are seen.	3rd person	Plural	Present	Passive	**video**
5 We are praised.	1st person	Plural	Present	Passive	**laudo**
6 You (pl.) are caught sight of.	2nd person	Plural	Present	Passive	**conspicio**
7 They were able.	3rd person	Plural	Perfect	Active	**possum**
8 They put.	3rd person	Plural	Perfect	Active	**pono**
9 He is heard.	3rd person	Singular	Present	Passive	**audio**
10 They were.	3rd person	Plural	Perfect	Active	**sum**

6 marks for each question. Total: 60

Exercise 1.23

1 Don't abandon me, friends! (4)

2 Few old men fight in wars. (5)

3 There are many temples in the middle of the city. (5)

4 Flavia is wiser than Marcus, isn't she? (6)

5 Few young men are able to write well. (5)

Total: 25

Exercise 1.24

1 cives principes laudaverunt. (3)

2 senes tristes currebant. (3)

3 magnam turbam vidimus. (3)

4 milites fortes iter longum faciunt. (5)

5 dominus omnes servos verbis crudelibus terret. (6)

Total: 20

Exercise 2.1

The city of Troy had been captured by the Greeks.(3) Ulysses himself was very happy.(3) For it was he who(3) had ordered the Greeks to build the wooden horse.(4) Now he said these words to his comrades:(4) 'Friends, the Greek race is very lucky.(4) We are loved by the gods.(4) Troy was captured by us, wasn't it?(4) Its walls were destroyed by us;(3) its temples were destroyed by us;(3) almost all the chieftains of the Trojans were killed by us.(5) A lot of money has been taken by us.(4) We have many prizes.(3) Helen, who is greatly loved by Menelaus,(5) is now being led back to Greece.(3) Believe me, friends!(3) – we will soon all return to Greece.(4) We will soon see our wives and our sons and our daughters again!'(11)

For a long time however Ulysses did not see his wife, named Penelope.(6) Nor did he see his son, named Telemachus.(4) For many years he wandered across the seas with his comrades(4) and underwent very great dangers.(3)

Total: 90

Exercise 2.2

1 (a) laetissimus/felicissima/maxima.   (1)

   (b) paene/magnopere/nunc/mox/iterum/diu.   (1)

   (c) redibimus/videbimus.   (1)

2 Accusative.   Object of the verb.   (2)

3 3rd.   Singular.   Pluperfect.   **iubeo**.   (4)

4 **maria** comes from **mare**, meaning 'sea', and *marine* mean something to do with the sea. (1)

Total: 10

Exercise 2.3

1 monitus, -a, -um

2 rectus, -a, -um

3 auditus, -a, -um

4 portatus, -a, -um

5 interfectus, -a, -um

6 ductus, -a, -um

7 deletus, -a, -um

8 captus, -a, -um

9 vulneratus, -a, -um

10 missus, -a, -um

11 visus, -a, -um

12 victus, -a, -um

13 iactus, -a, -um

14 dictus, -a, -um

15 punitus, -a, -um

1 mark for each question. Total: 15

Exercise 2.4

1 He was killed.

2 She was killed.

3 We were killed.

4 They were killed.

5 You (s.) were wounded.

6 I was sent.

7 She was captured.

8 You (pl.) were captured.

9 We were punished.

10 They were heard.

11 He was seen.

12 She was seen.

13 They were seen.

14 We (f.) were carried.

15 They were conquered.

16 He was sent.

17 She was sent.

18 She was led.

19 It was said.

20 You (pl.) were warned.

2 marks for each question. Total: 40

Exercise 2.5

1 The boy was punished.

2 The boys were punished.

3 The girl was seen.

4 The girls were seen.

5 The temple was built.

6 The temples were built.

7 The Romans were conquered.

8 The soldier was wounded.

9 The missiles were thrown.

10 The old man was killed.

11 The town was attacked.

12 The towns were attacked.

13 The pupils were warned.

14 The pupil was warned.

15 The father was loved.

16 The mother was loved.

17 The words were heard.

18 Voices were heard.

19 The city was destroyed.

20 The light was seen.

3 marks for each question. Total: 60

Exercise 2.6

1 The master punished the slave. (3)

2 The slave was punished by the master. (5)

3 The poet sent a book. (3)

4 A book was sent by the poet. (5)

5 Soldiers attacked the town. (3)

6 The town was attacked by soldiers. (5)

7 The Romans killed the enemy. (3)

8 The enemy were killed by the Romans. (5)

9 I saw the girl. (3)

10 The girl was seen by me. (5)

Total: 40

Exercise 2.7

1 The king said many words. (4)

2 Many words were said by the king. (6)

3 The girls heard the voices of the soldiers. (4)

4 The voices of the soldiers were heard by the girls. (6)

5 The slaves soon prepared food. (4)

6 Food was soon prepared by the slaves. (6)

7 The Romans finally conquered the Greeks. (4)

8 The Greeks were finally conquered by the Romans. (6)

9 The boy greatly loved the girl. (4)

10 The girl was greatly loved by the boy. (6)

Total: 50

Exercise 2.8

1 The Romans were seen by the enemy. (5)

2 I was punished by the master. (4)

3 The girl was seen by the boy. (5)

4 The girls were seen by the boys. (5)

5 The temple was built by the citizens. (5)

6 The walls were attacked by the enemy. (5)

7 Many words were said by the old men. (6)

8 The arrow was thrown by the soldier. (5)

9 The slave was set free by the master. (5)

10 The gift was sent by mother. (5)

Total: 50

Exercise 2.9

1 The pupils were warned by the teacher. (6)

2 The slave was punished by the cruel master. (5)

3 The words were not heard by me. (6)

4 A shout was heard by the teacher. (5)

5 We were seen by the enemy. (4)

6 You (s.) were praised by the teacher. (4)

7 I was wounded by many arrows. (4)

8 The town was attacked by the Romans. (5)

9 Many citizens were killed by the soldiers. (6)

10 The city was captured by the Greeks. (5)

Total: 50

Exercise 2.10

1 liber scriptus est.

2 dona data sunt.

3 senex interfectus/necatus/occisus est.

4 pueri iussi sunt.

5 bella facta sunt.

6 libri lecti sunt.

7 navis mota est.

8 puella iussa est.

9 auxilium datum est.

10 nauta interfectus/necatus/occisus est.

3 marks for each question. Total: 30

Exercise 2.11

1 pecunia a domino data est.

2 multi libri a poeta scripti sunt.

3 nuntius a rege missus est.

4 liber a magistro lectus est.

5 servi a domino interfecti/necati/occisi sunt.

5 marks for each question. Total: 25

Exercise 2.12

1 dux magna praemia dabat. (4)

2 Romani multas gentes vicerunt. (4)

3 servus audax senem gladio interfecit/necavit/occidit. (5)

4 discipuli sapientes libros legunt. (4)

5 militem fortem laudo. (3)

Total: 20

Exercise 2.13

1 principes vobis credunt.   The chieftains believe you. (6)

2 clamores audivimus.   We heard the shouts. (5)

3 magna praemia militibus dant.	They give great rewards to the soldiers.	(8)
4 milites servos interfecerunt.	The soldiers killed the slaves.	(6)
5 servi a militibus interfecti sunt.	The slaves were killed by the soldiers.	(10)

Total: 35

Exercise 2.14

1 senex currebat.	The old man was running.	(4)
2 gens superatur.	The tribe is overcome.	(4)
3 vocem feminae audivi.	I heard a woman's voice.	(6)
4 servus malus punitus est.	The bad slave was punished.	(8)
5 servus a domino punitur.	The slave is punished by the master.	(8)

Total: 30

Exercise 2.15

1 They killed.	3rd person	Plural	Perfect	Active	interficio
2 He was believing.	3rd person	Singular	Imperfect	Active	credo
3 She was killed.	3rd person	Singular	Perfect	Passive	interficio
4 You (s.) drank.	2nd person	Singular	Perfect	Active	bibo
5 He was shouting.	3rd person	Singular	Imperfect	Active	clamo
6 They defend.	3rd person	Plural	Present	Active	defendo
7 They will defend.	3rd person	Plural	Future	Active	defendo
8 You (s.) stayed.	2nd person	Singular	Perfect	Active	maneo
9 We were watching.	1st person	Plural	Imperfect	Active	specto
10 They are carried.	3rd person	Plural	Present	Passive	porto

6 marks for each question. Total: 60

Exercise 2.16

1 amavit.	He loved.
2 amatus/amata/amatum est.	He/she/it was loved.
3 interficiunt.	They kill.
4 interficiuntur.	They are killed.
5 credebam.	I was believing.
6 ivimus/iimus.	We went.
7 puniveratis.	You (pl.) had punished.

8	cucurrit.	He ran.
9	videbant.	They were seeing.
10	conspexisti.	You (s.) caught sight of.

2 marks for each question. Total: 20

Exercise 2.17

1 Pupils are not often praised by teachers. (6)

2 We will depart from the city tomorrow. (4)

3 All the slaves were holding big swords. (5)

4 We are often punished by the cruel master. (5)

5 This gift is not very good, is it? (5)

Total: 25

Exercise 3.1

After ten years(3) the whole of the city of Troy had been taken by the Greeks.(4) The walls had been destroyed and the temples had been burned,(4) and many Trojans had not been able to escape.(5) Ulysses and his companions had departed from Troy(3) and were returning to Greece in their ships.(3) They sailed across the sea for many days.(3) Finally the ships of the Greeks were driven by a storm to the land of the Lotus Eaters.(6) Those who eat the Lotus fruit(4) want always to sleep and to stay in this land.(7)

Ulysses sent three sailors to the town of the Lotus Eaters.(5) He ordered these sailors to look for food and water and to return to the ships in four or five hours.(12) He himself meanwhile stayed with the rest of his companions near the ships.(6) They stayed there for many hours.(3) After seven hours however(3) the three sailors had not returned.(3) They were being held by the Lotus Eaters.(2) The situation frightened Ulysses.(2) He was worried.(2)

Total: 80

Exercise 3.2

1 (a) decem/tres/quattuor/quinque/septem.   (1)

  (b) effugere/dormire/manere/petere/redire.   (1)

  (c) post/a/ad/trans/in/cum/prope.   (1)

2 Pluperfect.   discedo.   (2)

3 Accusative.   After the preposition trans.   (2)

4 To sleep.   People sleep in a dormitory.   (2)

5 Masculine.   (1)

Total: 10

Exercise 3.3

1 We had been seen.

2 It had been moved.

3 She had been praised.

4 They had been killed.

5 We had been led.

6 You (s.) had been captured.

7 I had been sent.

8 He had been captured.

9 She had been captured.

10 We had been wounded.

11 It had been given.

12 It had been written.

13 It had been destroyed.

14 You (s.) had been asked.

15 He had been led.

16 You (pl.) had been punished.

17 We had been ordered.

18 She had been seen.

19 It had been announced.

20 He had been killed.

2 marks for each question. Total: 40

Exercise 3.4

1 Forces had finally been prepared. (4)

2 He had been wounded by spears. (3)

3 She had been wounded by spears. (3)

4 We had been praised by the teacher. (4)

5 All the walls had been destroyed by the enemy. (6)

6 I had been abandoned by my friends. (4)

7 You (pl.) had been overcome by the Romans. (4)

8 We had been heard by the teacher. (4)

9 They had been conquered by the Greeks. (4)

10 You (s.) had been set free by the master. (4)

Total: 40

Exercise 3.5

1 Helen had been captured by Paris. (5)

2 Helen had been led to the city of Troy. (6)

3 Ships had been prepared by the Greeks. (5)

4 Ships had been sent to the city of Troy. (6)

5 Troy had been attacked by the Greeks. (5)

6 Many men had been killed. (4)

7 A very big horse had been built by the Greeks. (6)

8 The horse had been put in the middle of the city by the Trojans. (8)

9 Many Trojans had been killed by the Greeks. (6)

10 The city had finally been captured. (4)

Total: 55

Exercise 3.6

1 liber scriptus erat.

2 discipulus punitus erat.

3 pueri moniti erant.

4 puella visa erat.

5 miles vulneratus erat.

6 navis aedificata erat.

7 arma collecta erant.

8 femina/mulier servata erat.

9 milites interfecti/occisi/necati erant.

10 templum deletum erat.

3 marks for each question. Total: 30

Exercise 3.7

1 puella a Graecis reducta erat.

2 servi a domino liberati erant.

3 murus a servis aedificatus erat.

4 cena ab ancilla parata erat.

5 Graeci a Romanis victi erant.

5 marks for each question. Total: 25

Exercise 3.8

1 magna tempestas navem delevit. (4)

2 ventus naves pepulit. (3)

3 milites multa praemia acceperunt. (4)

4 omnes pueri puellas pulchras amant. (5)

5 cibum et aquam/cibum aquamque petimus. (4)

Total: 20

Exercise 3.9

1 multi viri currebant. (3)

2 omnes magistri sapientes sunt. (4)

3 servus malus effugiebat. (3)

4 cives fugerunt. (2)

5 multae naves appropinquant. (3)

Total: 15

Exercise 3.10

1 magna tempestas navem delevit. (4)

2 clamores senem terruerunt. (3)

3 magister maximam vocem habebat. (5)

4 milites urbem mox occupaverunt. (4)

5 omnes equi cibum amant. (4)

Total: 20

Exercise 3.11

1 fratrem clarum habeo. (3)

2 omnes comites mortem timebant. (4)

3 cives fortes oppidum defendebant. (4)

4 rex opus difficile nuntiavit. (4)

5 lucem claram in itinere vidimus. (5)

Total: 20

Exercise 3.12

1 miles multa vulnera in proelio accepit. (6)

2 principes Romani in urbe convenerunt. (5)

3 servi audaces ex oppido currebant. (5)

4 dominus crudelis senem tristem necavit/interfecit/occidit. (5)

5 iuvenes miseri sine mora discesserunt. (4)

Total: 25

Exercise 3.13

1 Storms often destroy ships. (4)

2 Wise pupils never believe their teachers. (5)

3 The Romans conquered many races. (4)

4 Cruel masters are never liked by slaves. (6)

5 Many slaves had already escaped from the town. (6)

Total: 25

Exercise 3.14

1 Don't punish that good slave, master! (6)

2 Not all the ships were destroyed in that storm, were they? (8)

3 The very wise old men will never be able to do this. (6)

4 Young men often seek great rewards. (5)

5 The Romans therefore destroyed the whole city. (5)

Total: 30

Exercise 3.15

1 The general praised the courage of all the citizens. (5)

2 The teacher gave many gifts to the wise pupils. (6)

3 That bad slave will be warned by this master tomorrow. (8)

4 Few old men are wise. (4)

5 The sailors had never seen a more savage storm than that one. (7)

Total: 30

Exercise 3.16

1 With the help of the Romans we will soon seize the whole city. (6)

2 Many of the Greeks were killed in that battle. (7)

3 Very many citizens met near the temple of Jupiter. (6)

4 A few old men had been abandoned in the city. (6)

5 No one is wiser than I. (5)

Total: 30

Exercise 3.17

1	pepuli.	I drove.
2	interfecerunt.	They killed.
3	convenistis.	You (pl.) met.
4	duxisti.	You (s.) led.
5	potuit.	He was able.

2 marks for each question. Total: 10

Exercise 3.18

1	portatur.	He is carried.
2	videmus.	We see.
3	mittebas.	You (s.) were sending.
4	ducti/ductae/ducta sunt.	They were led.
5	cucurrit.	He ran.
6	scripsi.	I wrote.
7	eratis.	You (pl.) were.
8	iaciebat.	He was throwing.
9	vincimus.	We conquer.
10	appropinquabant.	They were approaching.

2 marks for each question. Total: 20

Exercise 3.19

1 You (s.) were chosen.	2nd person	Singular	Perfect	Passive	eligo
2 They wrote.	3rd person	Plural	Perfect	Active	scribo
3 He caught sight of.	3rd person	Singular	Perfect	Active	conspicio
4 We are set free.	1st person	Plural	Present	Passive	libero

5 He went.	3rd person	Singular	Perfect	Active	**eo**
6 They were able.	3rd person	Plural	Imperfect	Active	**possum**
7 He was conquered.	3rd person	Singular	Perfect	Passive	**vinco**
8 We were hurrying.	1st person	Plural	Imperfect	Active	**festino**
9 We will arrive.	1st person	Plural	Future	Active	**advenio**
10 They were.	3rd person	Plural	Perfect	Active	**sum**

6 marks for each question. Total: 60

Exercise 3.20

1 urbes oppugnatae sunt.	The cities were attacked.
2 libri leguntur.	The books are read.
3 servi liberati erant.	The slaves had been set free.
4 oppida defenduntur.	The towns are defended.
5 senes interfecti sunt.	The old men were killed.

6 marks for each question. Total: 30

Exercise 3.21

1 puer punitus est.	The boy was punished.
2 senex relinquitur.	The old man is abandoned.
3 navis parata erat.	The ship had been prepared.
4 miles vulneratur.	The soldier is wounded.
5 femina spectatur.	The woman is being watched.

6 marks for each question. Total: 30

Exercise 3.22

1 Very many ships were built by the Romans. (7)

2 I will give a gift to my father tomorrow. (5)

3 Will you come with me? (4)

4 I read a good book yesterday. (4)

5 This book was very long. (5)

Total: 25

Exercise 4.1

Ulysses and his companions stayed near the ships for many hours.(7) The three sailors who had been sent to the Lotus Eaters had not returned.(5) Finally the worried Ulysses decided to look for the sailors.(5) He said these words to his companions:(4)

'I am worried.(2) Our friends have not returned.(3) They have been away for a long time.(2) Perhaps they are being held by the Lotus Eaters.(3) I want to look for them.(3) Who wants to come with me?'(4)

His companions looked at each other.(3) Then they shouted:(2) 'We do not want to stay here.(3) We all want to go with you.(4) Our friends will soon be set free by us.'(5) When Ulysses heard these words(4) he was happy.(2) He left a few companions near the ships(5) and said to them, 'Guard the ships well!(5) I and the rest will return in a few hours.(5) We will soon find the sailors.'(3)

Ulysses and his companions(2) hurried to the town of the Lotus Eaters.(3) They soon found the sailors, who were being held by the Lotus Eaters.(5) But when they saw them, they were amazed.(6)

Total: 95

Exercise 4.2

1 (a) missi erant. (1)

  (b) tandem/diu/fortasse/deinde/hic/mox/bene/ubi. (1)

  (c) custodite! (1)

  (d) liberabuntur/redibimus/inveniemus. (1)

2 Neuter. (1)

3 3rd.   Plural.   absum. (3)

4 Accusative.   After the preposition prope. (2)

Total: 10

Exercise 4.3

1 We want.

2 He does not want.

3 He wanted.

4 They wanted.

5 He did not want.

6 They did not want.

7 You (pl.) do not want.

8 He wanted.

9 They wanted.

10 You (s.) want.

11 You (s.) will not want.

12 To want.

13 They will want.

14 He did not want.

15 You (pl.) wanted.

16 You (s.) do not want.

17 To refuse/to be unwilling.

18 They do not want.

19 He will want.

20 They did not want.

1 mark for each question. Total: 20

Exercise 4.4

1 They did not want to stay. (2)

2 They wanted to depart. (2)

3 Do you (s.) want to go with me? (4)

4 We do not want to escape. (2)

5 I wanted to laugh. (2)

6 He wants to be wise. (3)

7 He does not want to do this. (4)

8 I do not want to work. (2)

9 I want to play. (2)

10 He did not want to sing. (2)

Total: 25

Exercise 4.5

1 The Greeks wanted to attack Troy. (4)

2 These pupils never want to work. (5)

3 Ulysses wanted to return to Greece. (5)

4 This boy does not want to work. (5)

5 The soldiers however did not want to do this. (5)

6 The boy did not want to listen to the teacher. (4)

7 Helen did not want to go to the city of Troy. (6)

8 All pupils want to be wise. (5)

9 The Romans wanted to conquer many races. (5)

10 A good teacher does not want to frighten his pupils. (6)

Total: 50

Exercise 4.6

1 For many years.

2 For a few hours.

3 For many days.

4 For a few days.

5 For five hours.

6 For the whole day.

7 For many hours.

8 For two hours.

9 For three days.

10 For six years.

2 marks for each question. Total: 20

Exercise 4.7

1 In a few hours.

2 On the third day.

3 At the tenth hour.

4 At that time.

5 On the fourth day.

6 On that day.

7 In eight days.

8 In a few days.

9 In four years.

10 In the sixth year.

2 marks for each question. Total: 20

Exercise 4.8

1 I will come in a few days. (3)

2 I slept the whole day. (3)

3 I was running for many hours; now I am tired. (6)

4 I will return in a few years. (3)

5 We worked for seven days. (3)

6 They arrived in the fourth year. (3)

7 We will depart in a few hours. (3)

8 I saw him at the third hour. (4)

9 He did not sleep for many hours. (4)

10 I will work for many days. (3)

Total: 35

Exercise 4.9

1 Many ships were prepared by the Greeks in a few days. (8)

2 The sailors sailed across the sea for many days. (6)

3 The Greeks attacked Troy for many years. (5)

4 The Greeks finally captured Troy in the tenth year. (6)

5 The Trojans fought against the Greeks for many hours. (6)

6 The walls were destroyed in a few hours. (5)

7 All the Greeks departed in five days. (5)

8 Ulysses wandered across the sea for many years. (6)

9 Ulysses ordered the sailors to return in a few hours. (6)

10 The sailors wanted to stay with the Lotus Eaters for many days. (7)

Total: 60

Exercise 4.10

1 laborare volo. (2)

2 ludere nolo. (2)

3 ridere volumus. (2)

4 cantare volebant. (2)

5 effugere volebam. (2)

6 nemo laborare vult. (3)

7 hodie venire nolebamus. (3)

8 festinare vis, Sexte. (3)

9 visne festinare? (3)

10 nunc/iam dormire vult. (3)

Total: 25

Exercise 4.11

1 servi effugere semper volunt.

2 heri discipuli laborare nolebant.

3 ille puer hoc facere nolet.

4 milites bene pugnare volebant.

5 senes currere saepe nolunt.

4 marks for each question. Total: 20

Exercise 4.12

1 cives urbem bene defendere volebant.

2 dominus bonus servos custodire vult.

3 pauci discipuli bene laborare volunt.

4 hostes muros statim oppugnare volebant.

5 servi dominum crudelem occidere/ necare/interficere volent.

5 marks for each question. Total: 25

Exercise 4.13

1 vult.   He wants.

2 custodiuntur.   They are guarded.

3 miserunt.   They sent.

4 missi/missae/missa sunt.   They were sent.

5 vis.   You (s.) want.

6	contendimus.	We hurried/marched.
7	ibas.	You (s.) were going.
8	poterat.	He was able.
9	cucurreratis.	You (pl.) had run.
10	fuerunt.	They were.

2 marks for each question. Total: 20

Exercise 4.14

1 He is killed.	3rd person	Singular	Present	Passive	interficio
2 They hurried.	3rd person	Plural	Perfect	Active	contendo
3 He was driven.	3rd person	Singular	Perfect	Passive	pello
4 I will depart.	1st person	Singular	Future	Active	discedo
5 They went.	3rd person	Plural	Perfect	Active	eo
6 They drove.	3rd person	Plural	Perfect	Active	pello
7 He wanted.	3rd person	Singular	Imperfect	Active	volo
8 He had been seen.	3rd person	Singular	Pluperfect	Passive	video
9 He stood.	3rd person	Singular	Perfect	Active	sto
10 We stayed.	1st person	Plural	Perfect	Active	maneo

6 marks for each question. Total: 60

Exercise 4.15

1	laborare nolo.	I do not want to work.	(1 + 2)
2	custos servum necabat.	The guard was killing the slave.	(3 + 3)
3	oppidum a milite occupatum est.	The town was seized by the soldier.	(4 + 5)
4	miles bene pugnavit.	The soldier fought well.	(2 + 3)
5	praemium militi saepe datur.	A prize is often given to the soldier.	(3 + 4)

Total: 30

Exercise 4.16

1	milites contendebant.	The soldiers were marching/ hurrying.	(2 + 2)
2	malos custodes non amamus.	We do not like the wicked guards.	(3 + 4)
3	opera difficilia numquam facimus.	We never do difficult tasks.	(3 + 4)
4	hae gentes superatae sunt.	These tribes were overcome.	(4 + 4)
5	tempestates naves ad insulas pepulerunt.	Storms drove the ships to the islands.	(4 + 5)

Total: 35

Exercise 4.17

1 multos dies laborabo.

2 omnem noctem dormivi.

3 quattuor diebus veniemus.

4 secunda hora advenit.

5 quarto die venerunt.

3 marks for each question. Total: 15

Exercise 4.18

1 Graeci urbem novem annos oppugnaverunt. (5)

2 decimo anno urbs a Graecis capta est. (6)

3 nuntius urbem quarto die conspexit. (5)

4 Ulixes in insula multos dies mansit. (6)

5 illa nocte multas puellas pulchras in oppido vidi. (8)

Total: 30

Exercise 4.19

1 We are building a temple to the gods. (4)

2 I have a son and a daughter. I love them. (8)

3 The general decides/decided to send a messenger to the enemy. (6)

4 With the help of the allies we seized the city. (5)

5 Because I am wise, I know everything. (7)

Total: 30

Exercise 4.20

1 servus cives nobiles custodiebat. (4)

2 senes oppidum gladiis longis defendebant. (5)

3 servi sapientes dominos non necant/occidunt/interficiunt. (5)

4 custodem vidimus. (2)

5 uxor mea villas amat. (4)

Total: 20

Exercise 5.1

Ulysses, looking for the sailors,(2) had arrived at the town of the Lotus Eaters.(3) The sailors were being held by the Lotus Eaters.(2) When Ulysses saw them, he was amazed.(4) For they were half asleep(3) and did not want to move themselves.(3)

'What are you doing?'(2) Ulysses asked them angrily.(3) 'What have you done?'(2)

The sailors replied to him: (3) 'Don't be angry, Ulysses.(3) We have eaten the lotus fruit.(2) The lotus fruit is very good.(2) We love it.(2) We want to stay here and sleep.(4) We don't want to go home.(2) Leave us here!'(3)

Ulysses however did not want to do this.(4) He therefore said to the sailors: 'I don't want to do this.(6) You will be carried to the ships immediately.'(3) Then he shouted to his companions:(3) 'Bring ropes!(2) Tie these sailors up with ropes!(3) Then carry them to the ships!'(4) The companions of Ulysses did the things which he had ordered.(4) They tied the sailors up with ropes.(3) The sailors, tied up with these ropes(3) and shouting loudly,(2) were carried to the ships.(3)

Total: 85

Exercise 5.2

1 (a) advenerat/iusserat.	(1)
(b) movere/esse/manere/dormire/ire/facere.	(1)
(c) noli/relinque/ferte/vincite.	(1)
2 is.	(1)
3 Nominative.	(1)
4 bonus.	(1)
5 Accusative. After the preposition ad.	(2)
6 iubeo.	(1)
7 He is a tightrope walker. ambulo = I walk, funis = rope.	(1)

Total: 10

Exercise 5.3

1 You (s.) carry.

2 He will be carried.

3 He carried.

4 To carry.

5 I carried.

6 They carried.

7 They were carried.

8 He was carried.

9 He carries.

10 We will carry.

11 He was carrying.

12 He was being carried.

13 They will carry.

14 They carry.

15 We had carried.

1 mark for each question. Total: 15

Exercise 5.4

1 The slave had carried much food.	(4)
2 I will carry/bring a lot of money tomorrow.	(4)
3 What are you (s.) carrying?	(2)
4 The soldiers are carrying weapons.	(3)
5 Weapons were being carried by the slaves.	(4)
6 What will be carried by the slaves tomorrow?	(5)
7 Food will be carried into the villa by the slaves tomorrow.	(7)
8 Swords were carried by the soldiers.	(5)
9 What was the slave carrying?	(3)
10 The slave was carrying a body.	(3)

Total: 40

Exercise 5.5

1 They were being carried.

2 They were sent.

3 I will be heard.

4 I was wounded.

5 We were being ruled.

6 They had been killed.

7 I will be feared.

8 I was punished.

9 We had been caught sight of.

10 They were killed.

11 We will be captured.

12 I will not be conquered.

13 We were being ordered.

14 We will be carried.

15 You (pl.) were led.

16 You (s.) are/will be sent.

17 They had been sent.

18 He is put.

19 He was killed.

20 She was killed.

21 It was being read.

22 I was called.

23 I will be called.

24 I was praised.

25 I am praised.

26 He was destroyed.

27 They were killed.

28 They were being prepared.

29 They were moved.

30 We are moved.

31 We had been attacked.

32 It was given.

33 It was announced.

34 They were seen.

35 It will be said.

36 They were being punished.

37 We were conquered.

38 They are heard.

39 We will be punished.

40 We are praised.

1 mark for each question. Total: 40

Exercise 5.6

1 Many spears were thrown by the soldiers in the battle. (8)

2 The temples of the city will soon be destroyed by the enemy. (6)

3 Our messengers were captured by the enemy. (6)

4 Money was given to the soldiers by the general. (6)

5 The money was received by the happy soldiers. (6)

6 The friend's money was given to the old man. (5)

7 Many lands are ruled by the queen. (5)

8 Many slaves were being led through the streets. (5)

9 The town had already been destroyed by the enemy. (6)

10 That general is not liked by many soldiers. (7)

Total: 60

Exercise 5.7

1 The king was killed by his brother. (5)

2 Boys are often warned by their fathers. (5)

3 Many prizes were given to the slaves. (5)

4 A long journey had been made by the soldiers. (6)

5 Many beautiful girls were seen by the boys in the street. (9)

6 The Romans will never be conquered by the enemy. (5)

7 This city was attacked by the enemy. (6)

8 Many soldiers were sent to the city of Troy. (7)

9 The boys are often punished by that teacher. (6)

10 Many soldiers were killed in the war. (6)

Total: 60

Exercise 5.8

1 The teacher is not liked by the boys. (5)

2 The soldier was wounded by a sword. (4)

3 Much food is being thrown into the river by the slaves. (7)

4 We are being attacked by the enemy! (3)

5 Many wounds had been received by the soldiers. (6)

6 This slave will be punished by the master tomorrow. (6)

7 Many words were said by the general. (6)

8 Money was given to the citizens by the king. (6)

9 The weapons of the enemy were captured by the Romans. (6)

10 The beautiful woman was caught sight of by the boy. (6)

Total: 55

Exercise 5.9

1 Who will be praised by the teacher tomorrow? (5)

2 Many pupils will be praised by the teacher tomorrow. (6)

3 Many horses were being led out of the fields. (5)

4 We will never be overcome by the Romans. (4)

5 A messenger was sent to the city. (5)

6 Boys are often punished by that teacher. (6)

7 Many ships had been prepared by the Greeks. (6)

8 This book will soon be read by me. (6)

9 Many weapons were given to the soldiers by the general. (7)

10 You (s.) are praised because you are brave, boy! (5)

Total: 55

Exercise 5.10

1 I am loved by all the girls. (5)

2 A big temple will be built on this mountain. (6)

3 Many enemies were conquered by the Romans. (6)

4 The master is feared by the slaves because he is cruel. (7)

5 Many Romans were wounded by arrows. (5)

6 A good dinner will be prepared by mother. (5)

7 The bad boy had been punished by the teacher. (6)

8 Money was found in the road by a boy. (7)

9 Many long roads were built by the Romans. (7)

10 The city of Troy was attacked by the Greeks. (6)

Total: 60

Exercise 5.11

1 After ten years the city of Troy was captured. (7)

2 Long words are not often said by small boys. (8)

3 Greeks are not often seen in Britain. (6)

4 Many words are often said by teachers. (6)

5 This danger was not seen by the slaves. (7)

6 Many fields were being destroyed by the enemy. (5)

7 That wounded horse was killed by the soldier with a spear. (8)

8 Many races were overcome by the Romans. (6)

9 The Greeks were finally conquered by the Romans. (6)

10 Many javelins had been made by the slaves. (6)

Total: 65

Exercise 5.12

1 iuvenes magna voce clamabant. (4)

2 fratrem clarum et sororem pulchram habeo. (6)

3 hostes appropinquabant. (2)

4 dominus crudelis omnes servos punivit. (5)

5 regina pecuniam amat. (3)

Total: 20

Exercise 5.13

1 ferris.

2 ferre.

3 latus est.

4 lata est.

5 feremur.

6 feretis.

7 tuleramus.

8 fert.

9 fertur.

10 ferebantur.

1 mark for each question. Total: 10

Exercise 5.14

1 servus cibum et aquam/cibum aquamque fert. (5)

2 milites gladios et scuta/gladios scutaque ferebant. (5)

3 cibus in villam a servis ferebatur. (6)

4 arma a militibus ferebantur. (4)

5 fer pecuniam et cibum, serve! (5)

Total: 25

Exercise 5.15

1	saepe laudamur.	We are often praised.	(1 + 2)
2	cives reginas amant.	Citizens like queens.	(3 + 3)
3	pueri puellas forte conspexerunt.	The boys caught sight of the girls by chance.	(3 + 4)
4	puellae amabantur.	The girls were being loved.	(2 + 2)
5	urbes mox occupabuntur.	The cities will be seized soon.	(2 + 3)

Total: 25

Exercise 5.16

1	custodiebar.	I was being guarded.	(1 + 1)
2	miles ducem laudat.	The soldier praises the general.	(3 + 3)
3	servus punietur.	The slave will be punished.	(2 + 2)
4	miles urbem cepit.	The soldier captured the city.	(3 + 3)
5	gladius a servo ferebatur.	The sword was being carried by the slave.	(3 + 4)

Total: 25

Exercise 5.17

1	He was carried.	3rd person	Singular	Perfect	Passive	**fero**
2	I went.	1st person	Singular	Perfect	Active	**eo**
3	He was.	3rd person	Singular	Imperfect	Active	**sum**
4	He had wounded.	3rd person	Singular	Pluperfect	Active	**vulnero**
5	He ordered.	3rd person	Singular	Perfect	Active	**iubeo**
6	They carried.	3rd person	Plural	Perfect	Active	**fero**
7	He was.	3rd person	Singular	Perfect	Active	**sum**
8	He was going.	3rd person	Singular	Imperfect	Active	**eo**
9	He is punished.	3rd person	Singular	Present	Passive	**punio**
10	You (s.) wrote.	2nd person	Singular	Perfect	Active	**scribo**

6 marks for each question. Total: 60

Exercise 5.18

1	auditis.	You (pl.) hear.
2	discesserunt.	They departed.
3	fui.	I was.

4 erat.

He was.

5 cantabant.

They were singing.

6 vulneramur.

We are wounded.

7 puniebatur.

He was being punished.

8 oppugnabantur.

They were being attacked.

9 mitteris.

You (s.) will be sent.

10 occisi/occisae/occisa sunt.

They were killed.

2 marks for each question. Total: 20

Exercise 5.19

1 omnes necabimur/occidemur/
  interficiemur.

2 urbs capietur.

3 puella spectabatur.

4 gladii ferebantur.

5 muri oppugnabuntur.

6 cibus consumebatur.

7 Romani vincentur/superabuntur.

8 pecunia colligebatur.

9 urbes defendentur.

10 omnia parabuntur.

2 marks for each question. Total: 20

Exercise 5.20

1 Look at that girl! I love her!

2 This boy has a famous father.

3 That storm destroyed many ships.

4 Flavia is the most beautiful of all girls.

5 Don't be afraid, citizens! Help will arrive.

5 marks for each question. Total: 25

Exercise 5.21

1 ab illo magistro semper amabar.

2 cibus ab illis ancillis parabatur.

3 puellae pulchrae a pueris
  spectabuntur.

4 navis ad insulam celeriter pellebatur.

5 hi servi a domino punientur.

5 marks for each question. Total: 25

Exercise 6.1

Shouting loudly,[2] the sailors who had eaten the Lotus fruit[3] were being carried out of the town of the Lotus Eaters to the ships by their companions.[5] When those who were guarding the ships[3] saw these men approaching,[4] they were very happy.[2] Ulysses himself, standing on the beach,[3] shouted to the guards:[2]

'These sailors were being forced by the Lotus Eaters to stay in this land.[6] They have eaten the lotus fruit.[2] They do not want to go home.[3] Throw them onto the ships![3] Depart quickly!'[2]

When the Greeks threw the sailors onto the ships,[4] they prepared everything quickly.[3] Having done this task[2] they were able to depart from the land of the Lotus Eaters in their ships, which were very quick.[6]

Total: 55

Exercise 6.2

1 (a) ferebantur/cogebantur. (1)

(b) manere/ire/discedere. (1)

(c) iacite/discedite. (1)

2 3rd.   Plural.   Pluperfect.   consumo. (4)

3 Ablative.   After the preposition ex. (2)

4 laetus. (1)

Total: 10

Exercise 6.3

1 This is the slave who works well. (6)

2 This is the maidservant who works well. (6)

3 This is the temple which is very big. (6)

4 These are the slaves who fled yesterday. (6)

5 These are the girls who sing well. (6)

6 That is the teacher whom I do not like. (6)

7 That is the beautiful girl whom I love. (6)

8 This is the wine which I often drink. (6)

9 Those are the slaves whom the master often punishes. (7)

10 The spears which I am carrying are long. (5)

Total: 60

Exercise 6.4

1 This is the good slave to whom I gave the money. (7)

2 These are the slaves to whom I gave the money. (6)

3 This is the girl whose father is famous. (7)

4 These are the slaves whose master is cruel. (7)

5 The villa in which I am living is small. (6)

6 These are the boys with whom I often play. (6)

7 The boy with whom I am playing is my friend. (6)

8 The words which the teacher said were bad. (6)

9 There is the villa from which many slaves escaped. (8)

10 The tall woman whom you see is frightened. (6)

Total: 65

Exercise 6.5

1 Menelaus, whose wife was Helen, was very famous. (7)

2 Paris, who was a Trojan chieftain, came to Menelaus. (8)

3 Paris decided to capture Helen, who was very beautiful. (7)

4 Paris led Helen to the city of Troy in a ship which was very fast. (11)

5 Menelaus, who was very angry, sent messengers to all the cities of Greece. (10)

6 The forces which Menelaus collected were great. (6)

7 Troy was a town whose walls were strong. (7)

8 Menelaus wanted to destroy Troy, which was a great city. (8)

9 The soldiers whom Menelaus praised were very brave. (6)

10 Helen, whom Menelaus loved greatly, was finally led back to Greece. (10)

Total: 80

Exercise 6.6

1 The slaves soon saw the master approaching. (5)

2 The sailors, shouting, were being carried to the ship. (5)

3 We never want to see women crying. (5)

4 We saw old men sitting in the temple. (5)

5 The soldiers, fighting bravely, were killed. (5)

6 The master was watching the slaves working in the fields. (6)

Chapter 6

7 The mother saw her son playing in the road. (6)

8 The mother saw her sons playing in the road. (6)

9 The king praised the citizens as they were defending the town. (5)

10 The farmer saw his horse running out of the field. (7)

Total: 55

Exercise 6.7

1 The boy saw the girl as she was going out of the villa. (6)

2 The slaves heard the master shouting again. (5)

3 The soldier, standing on the wall, was shouting in a loud voice. (7)

4 The soldiers, standing on the wall, were shouting in loud voices. (7)

5 The slave saw many horses as he was working in the fields. (7)

6 The slaves saw many horses as they were working in the fields. (7)

7 The father caught sight of his own daughter drinking wine. (6)

8 The master praised the maidservant as she was preparing dinner. (5)

9 The master praised the maidservants as they were preparing dinner. (5)

10 The cruel master killed the slave as he was escaping. (5)

Total: 60

Exercise 6.8

1 He was forced.	3rd person	Singular	Perfect	Passive	cogo
2 We are carried.	1st person	Plural	Present	Passive	fero
3 We will be carried.	1st person	Plural	Future	Passive	fero
4 They put.	3rd person	Plural	Perfect	Active	pono
5 They ruled.	3rd person	Plural	Perfect	Active	rego
6 They were able.	3rd person	Plural	Perfect	Active	possum
7 We had loved.	1st person	Plural	Pluperfect	Active	amo
8 We will be seen.	1st person	Plural	Future	Passive	video
9 They wanted.	3rd person	Plural	Perfect	Active	volo
10 They were running.	3rd person	Plural	Imperfect	Active	curro

6 marks for each question. Total: 60

Exercise 6.9

1 scripsit.	He wrote.
2 cogebamur.	We were being forced.
3 erat.	He was.
4 punitus/punita sum.	I was punished.

5 iistis/ivistis.	You (pl.) went.
6 videbuntur.	They will be seen.
7 audimus.	We are hearing/We hear.
8 spectaris.	You (s.) are being watched.
9 nolumus.	We do not want.
10 portabatur.	He was being carried.

2 marks for each question. Total: 20

Exercise 6.10

1 magistrum appropinquantem vidi.

2 feminas/mulieres clamantes audivi.

3 naves appropinquantes vidimus.

4 servum laborantem video.

5 servos festinantes vidi.

3 marks for each question. Total: 15

Exercise 6.11

1 magister appropinquans clamabat. (3)

2 dominus servum e villa currentem vidit. (6)

3 vir per viam ambulans puellam vidit. (6)

4 equos in agro currentes spectavimus. (5)

5 milites ex urbe effugientes interfecti/occisi/necati sunt. (5)

Total: 25

Exercise 6.12

1 Horses are loved by many girls. (5)

2 Nothing is better than the best wine. (6)

3 Marcus is a worse pupil than Sextus. (6)

4 We will all sail to the small island tomorrow. (6)

5 That beautiful girl is loved by many boys. (7)

Total: 30

Exercise 6.13

1 Graeci copias magnas colligebant. (4)

2 Romani urbem magnam armis oppugnaverunt. (5)

3 multae naves navigabant. (3)

4 duces boni milites fortes laudant. (5)

5 templa clara spectavimus. (3)

Total: 20

Exercise 7.1

Ulysses and his companions had escaped from the Lotus Eaters.(5) They sailed for many days and many nights.(4) Finally, driven by the winds and waves,(4) they arrived at land.(2) In the same land lived a race of giants.(4) The Greeks got off their ships(3) in order to prepare dinner on the beach.(3) Then they slept all night.(4)

At dawn/first light they got up from sleep.(4) When Ulysses and twelve friends collected their swords and javelins(7) they departed from the beach in order to look for food and water.(7) Soon they arrived at a cave in which there was a lot of food.(7) Having seen this food, the Greeks were very happy.(6) They decided to carry the food to the ships(4) in order not to die from hunger.(3) Ulysses ordered his friends to hurry.(5) However, while they were carrying the food to the ships,(4) the Greeks saw a huge giant approaching.(4)

Total: 80

Exercise 7.2

1 (a) quo. (1)

  (b) duodecim. (1)

  (c) appropinquantem. (1)

2 Ablative.   After the preposition e. (2)

3 3rd.   Plural.   Perfect.   **colligo.** (4)

4 Feminine. (1)

Total: 10

Exercise 7.3

1 The slaves were running in order to escape. (4)

2 The slaves were running in order not to work. (4)

3 The men escaped quickly in order not to perish. (5)

4 The men escaped in order not to be killed by the giant. (6)

5 The boys came to the city in order to see the queen. (7)

6 The citizens were fighting for a long time in order to defend the city. (7)

7 The teacher was reading many books in order to be wise. (7)

8 The teacher was shouting in order to be heard by the pupils. (6)

9 The slave was running in order not to be punished by the master. (6)

10 The Roman soldiers fought bravely in order to conquer the enemy. (8)

Total: 60

Exercise 7.4

1 Paris departed from the city of Troy in order to come to Menelaus. (9)

2 Paris captured Helen in order to lead her to the city of Troy. (9)

3 Menelaus asked for the help of his friends in order to collect great forces. (8)

4 Menelaus collected great forces in order to attack Troy. (7)

5 The Greeks attacked Troy in order to punish Paris. (6)

6 The Greeks fought bravely in order to capture the city. (6)

7 The Trojans fought bravely in order to save the city. (6)

8 The Trojans fought bravely in order not to be overcome by the Greeks. (7)

9 The Greeks finally built a huge horse in order to destroy the city. (8)

10 Many Trojans ran out of the city in order to escape from the danger. (9)

Total: 75

Exercise 7.5

1 puellae parvae noctes longas timebant. (5)

2 feminae/mulieres et senes/senesque effugiebant. (4)

3 principem clarum vidi. (3)

4 lux clara puellam terret. (4)

5 servus corpus mortuum fert. (4)

Total: 20

Exercise 7.6

1 3rd person	Plural	Imperfect	Subjunctive	Active	possum
2 3rd person	Plural	Perfect	Indicative	Active	colligo
3 3rd person	Singular	Perfect	Indicative	Active	duco
4 3rd person	Singular	Present	Indicative	Passive	moneo
5 1st person	Singular	Imperfect	Indicative	Active	terreo
6 3rd person	Singular	Imperfect	Subjunctive	Passive	interficio
7 3rd person	Singular	Pluperfect	Indicative	Active	intro
8 2nd person	Plural	Perfect	Indicative	Active	dico
9 3rd person	Singular	Present	Indicative	Active	fero
10 3rd person	Singular	Imperfect	Subjunctive	Active	vulnero

6 marks for each question. Total: 60

Chapter 7

Exercise 7.7

1 festinaret.

2 viderer.

3 legerent.

4 punireris.

5 essemus.

1 mark for each question. Total: 5

Exercise 7.8

1 iussit.   He ordered.

2 posuerunt.   They put.

3 stetimus.   We stood.

4 conspiciemur.   We will be caught sight of.

5 poterat.   He was able.

2 marks for each question. Total: 10

Exercise 7.9

1 fuerant.   They had been.

2 iimus/ivimus.   We went.

3 vis.   You (s.) want.

4 nolebas.   You (s.) did not want.

5 portatus/portata sum.   I was carried.

2 marks for each question. Total: 10

Exercise 7.10

1 discipuli laborabant ne a magistro punirentur.

2 senex cibum consumebat ut fortis esset.

3 pueri libros legebant ut sapientes essent.

4 venimus ut urbem novam spectaremus.

5 cucurri ne magister me ludentem videret.

6 marks for each question. Total: 30

Exercise 7.11

1 in eadem urbe laboramus.

2 non omnes eadem amant.

3 in eadem via habitant.

4 eosdem pueros heri vidi.

5 pecuniam eidem puellae dedi.

4 marks for each question. Total: 20

Exercise 7.12

1 idem vinum omnes amamus.

2 magistri eadem semper dicunt.

3 eidem pueri semper pugnant.

4 eundem servum iam punivi.

5 contra eosdem hostes pugnamus.

4 marks for each question. Total: 20

Exercise 7.13

1 cucurri ut mox advenirem. (4)

2 ad urbem venit ut reginam videret. (6)

3 servus currebat ut a domino effugeret. (6)

4 puer cucurrit ne a patre videretur. (6)

5 iuvenes ad urbem iverunt/ierunt ut puellas pulchras viderent. (8)

Total: 30

Exercise 7.14

1 noctes semper timemus. We always fear nights. (2 + 3)

2 milites audaces amamus. We love daring soldiers. (3 + 3)

3 hi milites bella amabant. These soldiers loved wars. (4 + 4)

4 duces a civibus laudabantur. The generals were being praised by the citizens. (3 + 4)

5 voces a custodibus auditae sunt. Voices were heard by the guards. (4 + 5)

Total: 35

Exercise 7.15

1 tandem captus est. He was finally captured. (2 + 3)

2 puellam pulchram spectat. He looks at the beautiful girl. (3 + 3)

3 filia a matre saepe monetur. The daughter is often warned by her mother. (3 + 5)

4 navis ad insulam pulsa est. The ship was driven to the island. (4 + 5)

5 senex a servo custodiebatur. The old man was being guarded by a slave. (3 + 4)

Total: 35

Exercise 7.16

1 You (s.) always have more money than I. (7)

2 We saw a big crowd of women in the city. (6)

3 Because I want to be wise, I am always reading books. (7)

4 I gave money to him yesterday. (4)

5 Many men are often killed in battles. (6)

Total: 30

Exercise 8.1

The Greeks saw this giant and were afraid of him.(4) They knew that they were now in great danger.(4) The name of this giant was Polyphemus.(3) He was very tall and very fierce and very arrogant.(3) He had one eye in the middle of his head.(3) When Ulysses saw Polyphemus approaching(4) he easily persuaded the Greeks to return to the cave.(4) He ordered them to hurry,(3) in order not to be caught sight of by Polyphemus.(3) The Greeks therefore hurried quickly to the cave.(3) They hid in the cave,(2) saying nothing and waiting for Polyphemus.(4) He himself soon arrived.(3) He entered the cave.(2) Then he shut the exit of the cave with a huge rock.(4) With this done, he made a fire.(3) By the light of the flames he caught sight of the Greeks.(4) The Greeks saw that Polyphemus was very angry.(4)

Total: 60

Exercise 8.2

1 (a) se. (1)

  (b) iam/facile/igitur/celeriter/mox/deinde. (1)

  (c) altissimus/ferocissimus/superbissimus/iratissimum. (1)

2 The infinitive. (1)

3 Accusative.   Object of the verb. (2)

4 3rd.   Singular.   Perfect.   facio. (4)

Total: 10

Exercise 8.3

1 The general ordered the soldiers to fight well. (4)

2 The general ordered the soldiers to attack the town. (3)

3 The general ordered the soldiers to defend the city bravely. (4)

4 The general ordered the soldiers not to be afraid of the enemy. (3)

5 The general ordered the soldiers not to be conquered by the enemy. (4)

6 The general ordered the soldiers to listen to the queen. (3)

7 The general ordered the soldiers not to sleep. (2)

8 The general ordered the soldiers to destroy the town. (3)

9 The general ordered the soldiers not to run. (2)

10 The general ordered the soldiers not to be captured. (2)

Total: 30

Exercise 8.4

1 The master persuaded the slave to work. (5)

2 The master persuaded the slave not to play. (2)

3 The master persuaded the slave to prepare the food. (3)

4 The master persuaded the slave to go to the city. (4)

5 The master persuaded the slave to read a book. (3)

6 The master persuaded the slave not to sleep. (2)

7 The master persuaded the slave not to be afraid. (2)

8 The master persuaded the slave to drink water. (3)

9 The master persuaded the slave not to drink wine. (3)

10 The master persuaded the slave to be good. (3)

Total: 30

Exercise 8.5

1 The general ordered the sailors to build ships. (6)

2 The general ordered the soldiers to fight bravely. (6)

3 The master warned the slave not to do this. (6)

4 The teacher often used to warn the pupils to work. (6)

5 Father warned me not to read that book. (7)

6 The master persuaded me to stay. (5)

7 The master ordered the slave to prepare dinner. (6)

8 I warned you not to be arrogant. (5)

9 The mother asked her son not to go to the city. (7)

10 The general ordered the soldiers to attack the town. (6)

Total: 60

Exercise 8.6

1 The queen persuaded the citizens to work well. (6)

2 The father warned his daughter not to play in the middle of the road. (8)

3 We asked the teacher to depart immediately. (5)

4 The general persuaded the soldiers not to be afraid of the enemy. (6)

5 The man persuaded his wife to go to the city with him. (8)

6 I warned him to do this immediately. (6)

7 The mother warned her daughter not to walk along the streets of the city at night. (9)

8 I ordered the boy to work. (4)

9 I persuaded father to give money to me. (6)

10 The wife persuaded the master to set that slave free. (7)

Total: 65

Exercise 8.7

1 milites superbi bella non timent. (5)

2 discipuli magistros crudeles non amant. (5)

3 multae naves appropinquabant. (3)

4 miles audax magna virtute pugnavit. (5)

5 servus effugiebat. (2)

Total: 20

Exercise 8.8

1	3rd person	Singular	Imperfect	Subjunctive	Passive	video
2	1st person	Plural	Imperfect	Subjunctive	Active	eo
3	1st person	Singular	Future	Indicative	Active	impero
4	1st person	Plural	Future	Indicative	Passive	voco
5	3rd person	Singular	Perfect	Indicative	Active	occido
6	3rd person	Singular	Imperfect	Subjunctive	Active	sum
7	1st person	Plural	Perfect	Indicative	Active	persuadeo
8	3rd person	Plural	Imperfect	Subjunctive	Active	defendo
9	3rd person	Singular	Perfect	Indicative	Passive	mitto
10	1st person	Plural	Imperfect	Indicative	Passive	voco

6 marks for each question. Total: 60

Exercise 8.9

1 facerent.

2 occideretur.

3 possemus.

4 portareris.

5 irent.

1 mark for each question. Total: 5

Exercise 8.10

1 constituam.   I will decide.

2 festinabamus.   We were hurrying.

3	dabitur.	It will be given.
4	tulit.	He carried.
5	cogebamini.	You (pl.) were being forced.
6	persuadebis.	You (s.) will persuade.
7	imperavi.	I ordered.
8	fugerunt.	They fled.
9	deletus/deleta/deletum est.	He/she/it was destroyed.
10	oppugnati/oppugnatae/ oppugnata erant.	They had been attacked.

2 marks for each question. Total: 20

Exercise 8.11

1 omnem discipulum rogavi ut laboraret.

2 discipulos sapientes rogavi ut laborarent.

3 puero persuasi ne hoc faceret.

4 pueris persuasi ne hoc facerent.

5 servo imperavit ut festinaret.

4 marks for each question. Total: 20

Exercise 8.12

1	dominus servis imperavit ut festinarent.	(5)
2	dux militi imperavit ut fortis esset.	(5)
3	dux militibus imperavit ut pugnarent.	(4)
4	magister discipulo imperavit ut laboraret.	(5)
5	puella matrem rogavit ut pecuniam servo daret.	(6)

Total: 25

Exercise 8.13

1	The girl whom I was looking at yesterday was very beautiful.	(6)
2	All the soldiers had been frightened by the words of the general.	(6)
3	We will run.	(1)
4	The son was forced to ask for help.	(5)
5	I know everything.	(2)

Total: 20

Exercise 9.1

The Greeks, shut in the cave, were afraid.(3) Ulysses knew that he and his companions were in great danger.(5) Polyphemus, having caught sight of the Greeks, was very angry.(4) He shouted in a loud voice:(2) 'This cave is mine, not yours.(4) Why are you present here?'(3)

Having heard these words, the Greeks gave up all hope.(4) Ulysses however advised his companions not to be afraid(4) and spoke these words to Polyphemus:(3) 'We are Greek soldiers.(2) The city of Troy was captured by us.(3) We are returning to Greece in order to see our families again.(5) Help us!(2) We seek food and water.(3) Give food to us, then we shall set off.'(5)

He, having heard this, said nothing.(4) He was a cruel animal.(3) He took two of the Greeks in his hand,(4) smashed their heads against a rock,(4) [and] immediately ate them.(3) The rest of the Greeks could do nothing.(5)

Total: 75

Exercise 9.2

1 (a) se. (1)

   (b) iuva/da. (1)

   (c) timerent/videamus. (1)

   (d) esse/facere. (1)

2 Ablative.   After the preposition a. (2)

3 3rd.   Singular.   Perfect.   **capio**. (4)

Total: 10

Exercise 9.3

1 The town was captured and destroyed./When the town was captured it was destroyed. (4)

2 The slaves were captured and punished by the master. (6)

3 The pupils were warned by the teacher and laughed. (5)

4 The slave was set free by the master and was very happy. (6)

5 The Greeks were conquered and captured by the Romans. (6)

6 The girl was abandoned by her friends and was crying. (5)

7 The soldiers were praised by the general and received rewards. (6)

8 Dinner was prepared by the maidservant and was praised by everyone. (8)

9 The land was captured by the Romans and was ruled well. (6)

10 The slaves were ordered to work by the master and were not happy. (8)

Total: 60

Exercise 9.4

1 Helen was seen by Paris and was led to the city of Troy./When Helen was seen by Paris she was led to the city of Troy. (9)

2 Many ships were prepared and sent to Menelaus. (7)

3 Troy was attacked by the Greeks and was defended by the citizens for a long time. (8)

4 The city was attacked for a long time and was finally captured. (6)

5 Many citizens were wounded by the enemy and fled from the city. (8)

6 A huge horse was built by the Greeks and abandoned near the city. (9)

7 The horse was abandoned near the city and seen by the Trojans. (8)

8 The horse was seen by the Trojans and was led into the city. (8)

9 Troy was captured by the Greeks and was finally destroyed. (7)

10 The ships were destroyed by a storm and never returned. (5)

Total: 75

Exercise 9.5

1 The boy saw the girl and loved her./When the boy saw the girl he loved her. (4)

2 The girl saw the boy and loved him. (4)

3 The man received the book and read it. (4)

4 The enemy attacked the city and captured it. (4)

5 The enemy captured the city and destroyed it. (4)

6 The Romans wounded the Greeks and killed them. (4)

7 The slave took the food and ate it. (4)

8 Menelaus prepared forces and sent them to the city of Troy. (7)

9 The Greeks saw Polyphemus and were afraid of him. (4)

10 The father punished his son and sent him out of the villa. (6)

Total: 45

Exercise 9.6

1 The allies prepared ships and sent them to Menelaus immediately./When the allies prepared ships they sent them to Menelaus immediately. (7)

2 The poet wrote a long book and sent it to all his friends. (8)

3 The Greeks built a huge horse and abandoned it near the city. (7)

Chapter 9

4 The Trojans saw the horse and led it into the city. (6)

5 The pupils didn't listen to the words said by the teacher. (7)

6 The soldiers prepared their javelins quickly and hurled them at the enemy. (7)

7 The Romans set free the slaves captured by the Greeks. (6)

8 Suddenly Polyphemus took two Greeks and ate them. (6)

9 I have already read this book which has been given to me. (6)

10 We praised the dinner prepared by the maidservant. (5)

Total: 65

Exercise 9.7

1 magnos clamores audivimus. (3)

2 dux iratus omnes milites malos punivit. (6)

3 hostes custodes armis occiderunt/necaverunt/interfecerunt. (4)

4 agricolae diem pulchrum amant. (4)

5 mater mea flet. (3)

Total: 20

Exercise 9.8

1 1st person	Singular	Future	Indicative	Active	venio
2 3rd person	Singular	Present	Indicative	Active	iuvo
3 3rd person	Plural	Perfect	Indicative	Active	scribo
4 3rd person	Singular	Imperfect	Subjunctive	Passive	servo
5 3rd person	Singular	Imperfect	Indicative	Passive	teneo
6 1st person	Plural	Imperfect	Subjunctive	Passive	vinco
7 1st person	Plural	Imperfect	Indicative	Active	pugno
8 1st person	Plural	Future	Indicative	Active	redeo
9 3rd person	Singular	Imperfect	Subjunctive	Active	sto
10 3rd person	Singular	Perfect	Indicative	Passive	trado

6 marks for each question. Total: 60

Exercise 9.9

1 vellet.

2 regereris.

3 nollent.

4 conspicerentur.

5 essemus.

1 mark for each question. Total: 5

Exercise 9.10

1	venient.	They will come.
2	risisti.	You (s.) laughed.
3	iuvabimur.	We will be helped.
4	pugnaverant.	They had fought.
5	vidit.	He saw.
6	sedebant.	They were sitting.
7	victus/victa sum.	I was conquered.
8	scripsi.	I wrote.
9	tradiderunt.	They handed over.
10	eramus.	We were.

2 marks for each question. Total: 20

Exercise 9.11

1 puella, a magistro irato punita, flebat. (6)

2 pueri, a patre visi, in agros cucurrerunt. (7)

3 miles, ab hostibus captus, interfectus/occisus/necatus est. (5)

4 naves, a Romanis paratae, statim discesserunt. (6)

5 arma, a servis collecta, nova erant. (6)

Total: 30

Exercise 9.12

1 dominus crudelis servum punitum interfecit/occidit/necavit.

2 discipuli magistrum visum non amabant/amaverunt.

3 milites custodes visos gladiis interfecerunt/occiderunt/necaverunt.

4 vocem puellae auditam statim amavimus.

5 vir librum lectum mihi dedit.

5 marks for each question. Total: 25

Exercise 9.13

1 Many races did not like the Romans. (5)

2 This farmer has more horses than that one. (7)

3 That city was being attacked by the enemy for a long time. (6)

4 The city of Troy was finally captured in the tenth year. (7)

5 The sailors will sail from the island today. (5)

Total: 30

Exercise 10.1

All the Greeks were very frightened.[4] They had now seen that Polyphemus was a very cruel animal.[5] Ulysses, who was the most daring of the Greeks,[4] decided to overcome Polyphemus by trickery.[4] Carrying a goblet full of wine,[3] he approached the giant.[2]

'Drink this wine, Polyphemus.[3] It is very sweet.'[2]

The giant took the wine and drank it immediately.[4] Then he shouted to Ulysses:[3] 'This wine is very good.[4] Give me more wine!'[3]

Ulysses gave him a second goblet, then a third, then a fourth.[7] Polyphemus was now drunk.[3] He suddenly fell to the ground and fell asleep.[4] When the Greeks saw that Polyphemus was sleeping,[4] they took a stake[2] and thrust it into the giant's eye.[3] He got up immediately,[2] shouting in a loud voice.[2] He was blind and very angry.[3] The Greeks wanted to escape from the cave.[4]

Total: 75

Exercise 10.2

1 (a) qui.   (1)

   (b) ferens/clamans.   (1)

   (c) secundum/tertium/quartum.   (1)

2 bonus.   (1)

3 3rd.   Singular.   Perfect.   do.   (4)

4 Accusative.   After the preposition ad.   (2)

Total: 10

Exercise 10.3

1 All farmers live in the country.   (4)

2 The general departed from Rome at first light.   (5)

3 Horses were running out of the fields.   (4)

4 We will go to the country tomorrow.   (3)

5 The boy left home and hurried to the city.   (7)

6 Many citizens used to live in Rome.   (4)

7 Slaves were hurrying from the country to Rome.   (4)

8 The father and his son were going home.   (5)

9 The soldiers will depart from Rome tomorrow.   (4)

10 The boy and the girl were staying at home.   (5)

Total: 45

Exercise 10.4

1 custodes celeriter cucurrerunt.   4 naves celeres erant.

2 tempestas maxima erat.   5 domus/villa parva est.

3 multa animalia currebant.

3 marks for each question. Total: 15

Exercise 10.5

1 principes cras convenient.   (3)

2 servi domum/villam custodiebant.   (3)

3 somnum amo.   (2)

4 servi praemia saepe petunt.   (4)

5 tempestas navem delevit.   (3)

Total: 15

Exercise 10.6

1 The slaves were forced to escape.   (4)

2 The animals were seeking food in vain.   (4)

3 Many ships were destroyed by that storm.   (6)

4 The master did not want to punish that slave.   (5)

5 The old man was walking along the roads for many days.   (6)

Total: 25

Exercise 10.7

1 Water was being carried into the villa by the slave.   (6)

2 Masters do not often believe slaves.   (5)

3 The city was being attacked by the enemy for many years.   (6)

4 Old men often do not want to work.   (4)

5 We do not all sing well.   (4)

Total: 25

Exercise 10.8

1 The soldiers killed many animals with arrows.   (5)

2 Many animals were killed by the soldiers with arrows.   (7)

3 The Greeks were attacking the city of Troy for many years, weren't they? (7)

4 Don't do this again, young man! (5)

5 The Greeks were better soldiers than the Trojans. (6)

Total: 30

Exercise 10.9

1 He will help.	3rd	Singular	Future	Active	iuvo
2 They persuaded.	3rd	Plural	Perfect	Active	persuadeo
3 He ordered.	3rd	Singular	Perfect	Active	impero
4 We were forced.	1st	Plural	Perfect	Passive	cogo
5 He had been carried.	3rd	Singular	Pluperfect	Passive	fero
6 He was being guarded.	3rd	Singular	Imperfect	Passive	custodio
7 He will want.	3rd	Singular	Future	Active	volo
8 We drove.	1st	Plural	Perfect	Active	pello
9 They looked for.	3rd	Plural	Perfect	Active	peto
10 I will kill.	1st	Singular	Future	Active	interficio

6 marks for each question. Total: 60

Exercise 10.10

1 nolumus.	We do not want.
2 coegit.	He forced.
3 lati/latae/lata sunt.	They were carried.
4 custodivisti.	You (s.) guarded.
5 volebant.	They wanted.

1 mark for each question. Total: 5

Exercise 10.11

1 petam.	I will seek.
2 pulsus/pulsa/pulsum est.	He/she/it was driven.
3 credidit.	He believed.
4 convenerunt.	They met.
5 poteras.	You (s.) were able.

1 mark for each question. Total: 5

Exercise 10.12

1 The teacher ordered the boys to work. (5)

2 The Trojans saw many Greeks approaching. (5)

3 The enemy were approaching in the middle of the night to attack the city. (7)

4 The son, warned by his father, did not do this again. (8)

5 We cannot all do everything. (5)

Total: 30

Exercise 10.13

1 Who saw the boy who did this? (6)

2 The city was being well defended by the citizens. (5)

3 The maidservants had been forced to prepare dinner by the master. (7)

4 Those soldiers whom you see are very brave. (6)

5 The general persuaded the soldiers to do this. (6)

Total: 30

Exercise 10.14

1 senes lente currebant.	The old men were running slowly.	(2 + 3)
2 tandem milites interfecti sunt.	Finally the soldiers were killed.	(3 + 4)
3 puellae a servis fortiter custodiebantur.	The girls were being guarded bravely by the slaves.	(3 + 5)
4 iuvenes pugnare nolebant.	The young men did not want to fight.	(2 + 3)
5 haec vina sunt quae amamus.	These are the wines which we like.	(5 + 5)

Total: 35

Exercise 10.15

1 animal effugiebat.	The animal was escaping.	(2 + 2)
2 templum deletum erat.	The temple had been destroyed.	(3 + 3)
3 ille dominus hunc servum punit.	That master is punishing this slave.	(5 + 5)
4 scutum a iuvene et servo portabatur.	The shield was being carried by the young man and the slave.	(4 + 6)
5 vir saepe sapientior quam mulier est.	A man is often wiser than a woman.	(4 + 6)

Total: 40

Exercise 10.16

1 multi viri in illo bello interfecti/occisi/necati sunt. (6)

2 puella pulchra a multis pueris spectabatur. (6)

3 multa vulnera a militibus in illo proelio accepta sunt. (8)

4 naves tempestatibus non saepe delentur. (5)

5 urbs a Graecis diu oppugnata erat. (5)

Total: 30

Exercise 10.17

1 soror amici mei equos amat. (5)

2 iuvenes audaces regem in urbe interfecerunt/occiderunt/necaverunt. (6)

3 servi corpora ex oppido ferebant/portabant. (5)

4 dominus pecuniam servis optimis tradet. (5)

5 copiae hostium Romanos vicerant. (4)

Total: 25

Exercise 10.18

1 propter moram multi servi vulnerati sunt.

2 milites a duce saepe laudabantur/ laudati sunt.

3 cibus servo a domino cras dabitur.

4 magistri a discipulis suis non saepe amantur.

5 multa arma prope urbem inventa erant.

6 marks for each question. Total: 30

Exercise 10.19

1 multi senes in viis clamabant. (5)

2 regina virtutem militis laudavit. (4)

3 servi regem bene custodient. (4)

4 pueri pecuniam in via non saepe inveniunt. (7)

5 senex multas feminas/mulieres pulchras amaverat. (5)

Total: 25

Exercise 10.20

1 You (s.) ought to run to the city quickly. (6)

2 She had been wounded by many arrows. (4)

3 Many friends will come with you soon. (5)

4 I order you to do this immediately. (5)

5 A very good dinner was being prepared by the woman. (5)

Total: 25

11

Exercise 11.1

The Greeks, having wounded Polyphemus, were afraid.(4) Polyphemus himself was very angry.(4) He knew that the Greeks wanted to escape from the cave.(5) Having removed the rock from the exit of the cave, he himself stood in the exit(7) in order to capture the Greeks as they were trying to escape.(5) However, he was not able to.(2) The Greeks, hanging below the bellies of the sheep, left the cave.(6) Having done this, they quickly ran to the ship.(5) They knew that they were now safe.(4)

The Greeks sailed for many days.(4) They finally arrived at the island of Aeolia.(4) Here lived Aeolus, king of the winds.(4) Ulysses asked him to give him and his companions help.(7) Aeolus, having put all the winds in a bag,(5) said these words to Ulysses: (3) 'Take this bag.(2) With the help of these winds you will be able to return to Greece.'(6) Having said these words,(3) Aeolus handed over the bag of winds to Ulysses.(4) Ulysses, having received the bag,(2) departed immediately from the island of Aeolia.(4)

Total: 90

Exercise 11.2

1 (a) iratissimus. (1)

   (b) effugere/velle/esse/redire. (1)

   (c) cape. (1)

   (d) ex/ab/in/sub/ad. (1)

2 Masculine.   Genitive. (2)

3 2nd.   Plural.   Future.   **possum**. (4)

Total: 10

Exercise 11.3

1 When the shout had been heard ...

2 When the girls had been frightened ...

3 When the town had been captured ...

4 When the city had been destroyed ...

5 When the enemy had been conquered ...

6 When the wall had been built ...

7 When my mother had been called ...

8 When the crowd had been ordered to depart ...

9 When the gift had been received ...

10 When the money had been handed over ...

11 When the weapons had been prepared ...

12 When a long book had been written ...

13 When these words had been heard ...

14 When the miserable inhabitants had been saved …

15 When the city had been defended well …

16 When the weapons had been collected …

17 When the girl had been seen in the road …

18 When the pupils had been punished …

19 When many soldiers had been wounded …

20 When the wall had been attacked …

2 marks for each question. Total: 40

Exercise 11.4

1 When the teacher had punished the pupil, he laughed. (4)

2 When many slaves had been set free, the master was happy. (6)

3 When the boy had caught sight of the very beautiful girl, he was very happy. (6)

4 When she had said these words, the queen departed. (5)

5 When the girl had heard this, she was very afraid. (5)

6 When the slaves had seen the savage master, they were afraid. (5)

7 When they had eaten the food, the sailors slept. (4)

8 When they had prepared their weapons, the soldiers charged, shouting. (5)

9 When she had read this book, the girl was sad. (6)

10 When they had conquered the enemy, the Romans departed. (4)

Total: 50

Exercise 11.5

1 When Helen had been captured, King Menelaus was very angry. (6)

2 When messengers had been sent to many cities, Menelaus collected great forces. (9)

3 When great forces had been collected, Menelaus was happy. (6)

4 When all the ships had been prepared, the Greeks sailed to Troy. (6)

5 When Troy had been attacked for ten years, the Greeks were tired. (7)

6 When the city had been well defended for a long time, the Trojan citizens were happy. (8)

7 When a big horse had been built, the Greeks departed in their ships. (7)

8 When the big horse had been led into the city, the citizens were very happy. (8)

9 When many citizens had been killed, the Greeks quickly captured the city. (7)

10 When the city had been captured, the Greeks returned to Greece. (6)

Total: 70

Exercise 11.6

1 hostes urbem occupaverunt. (3)

2 cives urbem magna virtute defendebant. (5)

3 pater pueri magnopere timet. (4)

4 servus ex oppido effugiebat. (4)

5 milites in proelio longo pugnaverunt. (4)

Total: 20

Exercise 11.7

1 magister a discipulis amatur. (4)

2 servi a domino puniti sunt. (4)

3 puellae pulchrae a pueris spectabantur. (5)

4 multi milites in proelio interfecti/occisi/necati sunt. (5)

5 templa delentur. (2)

Total: 20

Exercise 11.8

1 milite punito ...

2 hostibus visis ...

3 navibus aedificatis ...

4 senibus auditis ...

5 Romanis victis ...

6 libro lecto ...

7 custodibus interfectis/occisis/necatis ...

8 urbe capta ...

9 viris fortibus laudatis ...

10 auro invento ...

2 marks for each question. Total: 20

Exercise 11.9

1	3rd person	Singular	Present	Indicative	Passive	oppugno
2	3rd person	Singular	Perfect	Indicative	Active	fleo
3	3rd person	Plural	Perfect	Indicative	Passive	iacio
4	3rd person	Plural	Perfect	Indicative	Active	do
5	3rd person	Singular	Imperfect	Indicative	Passive	laudo
6	3rd person	Singular	Imperfect	Subjunctive	Active	nuntio
7	3rd person	Singular	Pluperfect	Indicative	Active	facio
8	1st person	Singular	Future	Indicative	Active	effugio
9	3rd person	Singular	Perfect	Indicative	Active	intro
10	3rd person	Plural	Imperfect	Subjunctive	Active	do

6 marks for each question. Total: 60

Exercise 11.10

1 crederent.

2 defenderetur.

3 videretis.

4 vulnerarer.

5 relinqueremus.

1 mark for each question. Total: 5

Exercise 11.11

1	colligebantur.	They were being collected.
2	cupiebat.	He was wanting.
3	habuimus.	We had.
4	cucurrerant.	They had run.
5	poterat.	He was able.
6	dedimus.	We gave.
7	ibo.	I will go.
8	discesserunt.	They departed.
9	noluit.	He did not want.
10	capietur.	He will be captured.

2 marks for each question. Total: 20

Exercise 11.12

1 The Romans fought in many battles against the enemy. (7)

2 Romulus built a town on seven mountains. (6)

3 The name of this town was Rome. (5)

4 The Roman soldiers were better than the Greeks./The Romans were better soldiers than the Greeks. (6)

5 Many horses were wounded by the javelins of the enemy. (6)

Total: 30

Exercise 12.1

Ulysses, having received the bag of winds from Aeolus,[4] had departed from the island of Aeolia.[3] He was now finally approaching the island of Ithaca with his companions.[6] However, Ulysses' companions were not happy.[5] They did not know that winds were in the bag which had been given to Ulysses;[6] they believed that Ulysses had gold and money in the bag;[6] they said that Ulysses was a cruel and mean man.[6] They thought that Ulysses wanted to keep the gold and money.[6]

Therefore, while the tired Ulysses was sleeping,[5] his companions decided to open the bag.[4] With the bag opened,[2] all the winds immediately escaped from the bag[5] and drove the ship away from the island of Ithaca.[5] Ulysses, woken from his sleep,[3] was very angry when he had seen this.[4] He shouted:[1] 'Why did you do this?[3] We had almost arrived home.'[3] The ship was driven back to Aeolia.[4] King Aeolus however did not want to give help to the Greeks again.[7] They were able to do nothing.[4] They knew that Ulysses was very angry and that they had been stupid.[8]

Total: 100

Exercise 12.2

1 (a) sacco ... accepto/sacco aperto/hoc viso. (1)

(b) inesse/habere/esse/tenere/velle/aperire/dare/facere. (1)

(c) discesserat/adveneramus. (1)

(d) Ulixi/Graecis. (1)

2 Ablative. After the preposition cum. (2)

3 Present infinitive. volo. (2)

4 iratus. iratior. (2)

Total: 10

Exercise 12.3

1 I see that the boy is running.

2 I see that the boys are running.

3 I saw that the boy was running.

4 I saw that the boys were running.

5 I hear that the girl is shouting.

6 I hear that the girls are shouting.

7 I heard that the girl was shouting.

8 I heard that the girls were shouting.

9 I know that the soldiers are coming.

10 I knew that the soldiers were coming.

3 marks for each question. Total: 30

Exercise 12.4

1 I know that this slave is escaping.   (4)

2 I know that these slaves are escaping.   (4)

3 I knew that this slave was escaping.   (4)

4 I knew that these slaves were escaping.   (4)

5 I see that all the pupils are working.   (4)

6 I saw that all the pupils were working.   (4)

7 The teacher knows that the boy is not working.   (5)

8 The teacher knew that the boy was not working.   (5)

9 The father knows that his son likes money.   (5)

10 The pupils knew that this teacher was good.   (6)

Total: 45

Exercise 12.5

1 I know that the farmer is working.   (3)

2 I know that the farmers are working.   (3)

3 I knew that the farmer was working.   (3)

4 I knew that the farmers were working.   (3)

5 The boy says that the girl is beautiful.   (5)

6 The boy says that the girls are beautiful.   (5)

7 The boy said that the girl was beautiful.   (5)

8 The boy said that the girls were beautiful.   (5)

9 I hear that the teacher is good.   (4)

10 I heard that the teacher was good.   (4)

Total: 40

Exercise 12.6

1 We know that all teachers are wise.   (5)

2 I see that you are finally working well.   (5)

3 I hear that the girl is coming.   (3)

4 They say that the Romans are attacking the town.   (4)

5 The slaves know that the master is already approaching.   (5)

6 The general knows that the soldiers are brave.   (5)

7 The teachers know that all the girls are working well.   (6)

8 We know that that man has a loud voice. (6)

9 I hear that many slaves are escaping. (4)

10 Marcus knows that Flavia always prepares good dinners. (7)

Total: 50

Exercise 12.7

1 The general ordered many javelins to be thrown. (5)

2 The citizens wanted the city to be defended well. (5)

3 We do not want to be captured by the enemy. (4)

4 The general ordered the citizens to be guarded by slaves. (6)

5 The master ordered this slave to be killed. (5)

6 The Romans never wanted to be conquered by the enemy. (6)

7 The chieftain ordered weapons to be collected by the citizens. (6)

8 The king ordered money to be handed over to the enemy. (5)

9 The Greeks ordered a new city to be built in this place. (8)

10 Pupils do not want to be punished by the teacher. (5)

Total: 55

Exercise 12.8

1 The Trojans saw that their own city was being attacked by the Greeks. (7)

2 The Trojans saw that they were being conquered by the Greeks. (6)

3 The Trojan citizens knew that the city was being captured. (5)

4 The king saw that the temples of Troy were being destroyed by the Greeks. (6)

5 The king saw that many citizens were being killed by the Greeks. (7)

6 The citizens did not know that a huge horse was being built by the Greeks. (7)

7 The Greeks saw that the horse was being led into the city by the Trojans. (8)

8 Ulysses heard that his companions were being held by the Lotus Eaters. (7)

9 Ulysses knew that he was being punished by the gods. (6)

10 Ulysses saw that his ships were being destroyed by the storm. (6)

Total: 65

Exercise 12.9

1 milites multa vulnera acceperunt. (4)

2 multae naves ad insulam navigabant. (5)

3 dux virtutem militum laudavit. (4)

4 nomen pueri nescio. (3)

5 senes magnis vocibus clamabant. (4)

Total: 20

Exercise 12.10

1 discipuli a magistris sapientibus laudantur. (5)

2 puniris, puer! (2)

3 multa arma a Romanis parabantur. (5)

4 puella bona a matre saepe laudabatur. (5)

5 multa corpora portabantur. (3)

Total: 20

Exercise 12.11

1	3rd person	Singular	Pluperfect	Indicative	Active	mitto
2	3rd person	Singular	Imperfect	Indicative	Active	scio
3	3rd person	Singular	Future	Indicative	Active	eo
4	1st person	Plural	Imperfect	Subjunctive	Active	possum
5	3rd person	Singular	Perfect	Indicative	Active	ludo
6	3rd person	Plural	Perfect	Indicative	Active	pereo
7	1st person	Plural	Imperfect	Indicative	Active	nescio
8	3rd person	Singular	Imperfect	Indicative	Active	possum
9	3rd person	Plural	Present	Indicative	Passive	rego
10	3rd person	Singular	Future	Indicative	Active	ostendo

6 marks for each question. Total: 60

Exercise 12.12

1 ferrem.

2 daretur.

3 occideremus.

4 parareris.

5 vellet.

1 mark for each question. Total: 5

Exercise 12.13

1 sciebas.   You (s.) knew.

2 cepit.   He took.

3 poterant.   They were able.

4 volebant.	They wanted.	
5 ducti/ductae/ducta sunt.	They were led.	
6 dicam.	I will say.	
7 fecerunt.	They made.	
8 iecisti.	You (s.) threw.	
9 videbimur.	We will be seen.	
10 effugerunt.	They escaped.	

2 marks for each question. Total: 20

Exercise 12.14

1 scio servum festinare.

2 scio servos festinare.

3 sciebam servum festinare.

4 sciebam servos festinare.

5 audio feminam/mulierem cantare.

6 audio feminas/mulieres cantare.

7 audiebam feminam/mulierem cantare.

8 audiebam feminas/mulieres cantare.

9 video naves venire.

10 vidi naves venire.

3 marks for each question. Total: 30

Exercise 12.15

1 omnes discipuli sciunt illum magistrum sapientem esse. (7)

2 rex vidit hostes muros delere. (5)

3 rex vidit muros ab hostibus deleri. (6)

4 Romani sciebant Graecos celeriter appropinquare. (5)

5 omnes sciebamus hunc senem ambulare non posse. (7)

Total: 30

Exercise 12.16

1 haec animalia amamus.	We love these animals.	(3 + 3)
2 corpora magna erant.	The bodies were big.	(3 + 3)
3 per vias longas itinera facimus.	We make journeys along long roads.	(4 + 5)
4 scuta a militibus portata sunt.	Shields were carried by the soldiers.	(4 + 5)
5 magistri superbi a discipulis non amabantur.	The arrogant teachers were not liked by the pupils.	(4 + 6)

Total: 40

Exercise 12.17

1 navis mox advenit.	The ship soon arrived.	(2 + 3)
2 tandem dux militi persuasit.	The general finally persuaded the soldier.	(3 + 4)
3 animal per viam currebat.	The animal was running along the road.	(3 + 4)
4 senex militem crudelem timebat.	The old man was afraid of the cruel soldier.	(4 + 4)
5 puella a puero saepe amatur.	The girl is often loved by the boy.	(3 + 5)

Total: 35

Exercise 12.18

1 What will we do tomorrow? (3)
2 I was sleeping for many hours. (3)
3 They captured the slaves and killed them. (3)
4 Many books were written by him. (6)
5 The master of those slaves is very cruel. (5)

Total: 20

Exercise 13.1

The Greeks soon arrived at the island of Aeaea.(5) Six sailors were sent by Ulysses into the middle of the island(6) in order to look for food and water.(4) They were away for many hours.(3) Finally one of them, Eurylochus by name,(4) returned alone to the rest.(4) The Greeks saw that Eurylochus was afraid.(4) Ulysses therefore ordered Eurylochus(3) to tell immediately what had happened.(4) Eurylochus replied as follows:(3)

'In the middle of the island we found a big house,(6) in which lives a very beautiful goddess, named Circe.(7) She ordered us to go into the house(5) in order to drink wine.'(3)

Eurylochus said that he alone had stayed outside the house,(7) but that the others had entered and had drunk the drug given by the goddess;(9) he said that the goddess, holding a stick in her hand, had changed them into pigs.(9)

Having heard this(2) Ulysses said to Eurylochus: 'You have done well.(5) I will go to the goddess's house immediately(4) in order to punish her(3) and save our companions.'(3) Having spoken these words,(3) Ulysses set out into the middle of the island.(4)

Total: 110

Exercise 13.2

1 (a) missi sunt. (1)

(b) qua. (1)

(c) se. (1)

(d) tenentem. (1)

2 Accusative.   Accusative of time 'how long'. (2)

3 Dative.   After the verb **impero**. (2)

4 I will go.   eo. (2)

Total: 10

Exercise 13.3

1 I hear that the messenger has arrived. (3)

2 I hear that the messengers have arrived. (3)

3 I heard that the messenger had arrived. (3)

4 I heard that the messengers had arrived. (3)

5 I know that that boy has done this. (5)

6 I know that those boys have done this. (5)

7 I knew that the boy had done this. (4)

8 I knew that the boys had done this. (4)

9 We knew that these soldiers had fought well. (5)

10 I see that the Greeks have finally captured Troy. (5)

Total: 40

Exercise 13.4

1 The messenger says that the enemy have captured the city. (5)

2 The messenger said that the enemy had captured the city. (5)

3 The messenger says that the city has been captured by the enemy. (7)

4 The messenger said that the city had been captured by the enemy. (7)

5 The teacher knows that all the pupils have worked well. (6)

6 The general knows that the soldier has received many wounds. (6)

7 I know that the Romans have conquered many races. (5)

8 I hear that you have read this book. (5)

9 That boy said that he had read many books. (7)

10 I know that these soldiers have fought bravely for three days. (7)

Total: 60

Exercise 13.5

1 The messenger said that the enemy had finally destroyed the city. (6)

2 The messenger said that the city had finally been destroyed by the enemy. (8)

3 The general knew that the soldiers had received many wounds. (6)

4 The general knew that many wounds had been received by the soldiers. (8)

5 We saw that the maidservant had prepared a good dinner. (5)

6 We saw that a good dinner had been prepared by the maidservant. (7)

7 I knew that that master had punished many slaves. (6)

8 I knew that many slaves had been punished by that master. (8)

9 The teacher said that all the pupils had read this book. (7)

10 The teacher said that this book had been read by all the pupils. (9)

Total: 70

Exercise 13.6

1 The Greeks knew that Helen had been led to the city of Troy by Paris. (10)

2 The Trojans saw that the Greeks had prepared many ships. (6)

3 The Greeks knew that the Trojans had defended the city well. (6)

4 The Greeks knew that the city had been well defended by the Trojans. (8)

5 The Trojans did not know that the Greeks had built a huge horse. (6)

6 The Trojans did not know that a huge horse had been built by the Greeks. (8)

7 The Greeks knew that they had conquered the Trojans. (5)

8 The Trojans knew that they had been conquered by the Greeks. (7)

9 The citizens saw that the Greeks had destroyed many temples. (6)

10 The citizens saw that many temples had been destroyed by the Greeks. (8)

Total: 70

Exercise 13.7

1 Ulysses knew that he had not seen his wife for a long time. (8)

2 Polyphemus saw that the Greeks had taken his food. (6)

3 The Greeks knew that they had been caught sight of by Polyphemus. (7)

4 The companions of Ulysses knew that they had been bad. (6)

5 The Greeks saw that Eurylochus was afraid. (4)

6 Eurylochus said that he had seen a very beautiful goddess in the middle of the island. (9)

7 Eurylochus said that the goddess lived in a big villa. (7)

8 Eurylochus said that he had been afraid of the goddess. (5)

9 The Trojans saw that the army of the Greeks was big. (6)

10 The Greeks believed that they were not able to capture Troy. (7)

Total: 65

Exercise 13.8

1 The general saw that the town was being attacked by the Romans. (6)

2 The man said that he had loved many beautiful women. (7)

3 The man said that many beautiful women had been loved by him. (9)

4 I hear that this book is very long. (5)

5 We saw that many horses were running out of the field. (6)

6 The soldiers saw that the enemy were approaching quickly. (5)

7 The general knew that the city had been captured by the enemy. (7)

8 I hear that the Greeks have captured Troy. (4)

9 I know that you want to read this book. (6)

10 The messenger announced that the Romans did not want to fight. (5)

Total: 60

Exercise 13.9

1 I know that I am the best pupil. (5)

2 The girl said that she was afraid. (4)

3 The girls said that they were afraid. (4)

4 Julius Caesar knew that he was a good general. (7)

5 The girl knew that she was beautiful. (5)

6 The soldiers said that they wanted to fight. (5)

7 All girls know that they are better than boys. (8)

8 The queen believed that she was a very beautiful woman. (6)

9 Menelaus announced that he wanted to punish the Trojans. (6)

10 Polyphemus said that he liked wine. (5)

Total: 55

Exercise 13.10

1 senes sapientes ab/ex urbe fugerunt. (5)

2 parentes puellae timebant. (3)

3 propter virtutem nostram hostes vicimus. (4)

4 servi corpora mortua ferebant/portabant. (4)

5 omnes opera facilia amamus. (4)

Total: 20

Exercise 13.11

1 nuntii ad urbem missi sunt. (4)

2 hastae/tela trans viam iactae/iacta sunt. (4)

3 rex malus ab hostibus victus est. (5)

4 multa arma a civibus colligebantur. (5)

5 senex interfectus/occisus/necatus est. (2)

Total: 20

Exercise 13.12

1 scio discipulum bene laboravisse. (4)

2 scio discipulos bene laboravisse. (4)

3 sciebam discipulum bene laboravisse. (4)

4 sciebam discipulos bene laboravisse. (4)

5 videmus navem advenisse. (3)

6 videmus naves advenisse. (3)

7 vidimus navem advenisse. (3)

8 vidimus naves advenisse. (3)

9 audivit puellam festinavisse. (3)

10 nesciebamus urbem iam captam esse. (4)

Total: 35

Exercise 13.13

1 milites sciebant tempestatem naves delevisse. (5)

2 nuntius nuntiavit exercitum victum esse. (4)

3 nautae sciunt navem e portu navigavisse. (6)

4 dux vidit multos milites vulneratos esse. (5)

5 audivimus hostes omnes cives interfecisse/occidisse/necavisse. (5)

Total: 25

Exercise 13.14

1 3rd person	Singular	Perfect	Indicative	Active	sum
2 3rd person	Singular	Imperfect	Subjunctive	Active	adeo
3 1st person	Singular	Pluperfect	Indicative	Active	nolo
4 3rd person	Plural	Perfect	Indicative	Active	conspicio
5 1st person	Plural	Imperfect	Indicative	Active	scribo
6 3rd person	Singular	Perfect	Indicative	Active	vinco
7 3rd person	Singular	Imperfect	Indicative	Passive	aedifico
8 3rd person	Plural	Imperfect	Subjunctive	Active	sum
9 3rd person	Singular	Imperfect	Indicative	Active	credo
10 1st person	Plural	Imperfect	Indicative	Active	sto

6 marks for each question. Total: 60

Exercise 13.15

1 iaceremus.

2 iuberentur.

3 irem.

4 laudaremini.

5 esset.

1 mark for each question. Total: 5

Exercise 13.16

1	nuntiavit.	He announced.
2	occisus/occisa/occisum est.	He/she/it was killed.
3	oppugnaveramus.	We had attacked.
4	pepulerunt.	They drove.
5	ferebatur.	He was being carried.
6	potuerunt.	They were able.
7	movebimur.	We will be moved.
8	miserunt.	They sent.
9	liberabitur.	He will be set free.
10	rogabamus.	We were asking.

2 marks for each question. Total: 20

Exercise 13.17

1 The master whom the slave feared was cruel. (6)

2 The slave was fleeing because he was afraid of the master. (5)

3 The general ordered the soldiers to seize the city immediately. (6)

4 The slaves often used to be punished by him. (5)

5 You (pl.) are going into the city. (3)

Total: 25

Exercise 14.1

When Ulysses had heard Eurylochus' words,(4) he set off into the middle of the island(3) to save his companions and punish Circe.(5) The frightened Eurylochus did not want to follow Ulysses.(4) Ulysses soon found the house of the goddess.(4) When he had entered the house(2) and had approached the goddess,(2) he spoke these words to her:(3)

'You are a wicked goddess, Circe.(3) I know that you have changed my companions into pigs.'(5) Having heard these words,(3) Circe replied to Ulysses:(2) 'Do not be angry, Ulysses.(3) Take this wine.'(3) She tried to give a drug to Ulysses, but in vain:(5) for he was protected by the gods.(4) Circe was afraid.(2) Since she knew that she was not able to turn Ulysses into a pig, she shouted:(8) 'You are a lucky man, Ulysses.(3) You are protected by the gods.(3) I will turn your companions back into human shape immediately.'(7) Having spoken these words,(2) Circe encouraged the Greeks(2) to stay with her for a long time.(3) The Greeks stayed on Circe's island for one year.(5)

Total: 90

Exercise 14.2

1 (a) servaret/puniret/sciret/manerent. (1)

 (b) se. (1)

2 Dative. (1)

3 Accusative.   Accusative of time 'how long'. (2)

Total: 5

Exercise 14.3

1 He tries.

2 You (s.) enter.

3 We set out.

4 I speak.

5 They follow.

6 He encourages.

7 We try.

8 They speak.

9 They try.

10 They enter.

1 mark for each question. Total: 10

Exercise 14.4

1 You (s.) try.

2 He sets out.

3 You (pl.) encourage.

4 I try.

5 He enters.

6 We encourage.

7 He speaks.

8 You (pl.) try.

9 You (pl.) set out.

10 I follow.

1 mark for each question. Total: 10

Exercise 14.5

1 You (pl.) enter.

2 You (s.) encourage.

3 You (pl.) speak.

4 You (s.) set out./You (s.) will set out.

5 You (s.) speak./You (s.) will speak.

6 You (pl.) follow.

7 I set out.

8 We enter.

9 They encourage.

10 I enter.

1 mark for each question. Total: 10

Exercise 14.6

1 He was following.

2 I was entering.

3 I was speaking.

4 I was encouraging.

5 We were trying.

6 We were setting out.

7 We were encouraging.

8 He was entering.

9 They were following.

10 He was speaking.

1 mark for each question. Total: 10

Exercise 14.7

1 You (pl.) were trying.

2 I was following.

3 You (s.) were entering.

4 They were speaking.

5 He was trying.

6 You (s.) were setting out.

7 You (pl.) were encouraging.

8 You (pl.) were speaking.

9 We were entering.

10 He was encouraging.

1 mark for each question. Total: 10

Exercise 14.8

1 You (s.) were encouraging.

2 They were entering.

3 They were trying.

4 He was setting out.

5 You (s.) were following.

6 You (pl.) were entering.

7 They were encouraging.

8 I was setting out.

9 You (s.) were trying.

10 We were speaking.

1 mark for each question. Total: 10

Exercise 14.9

1 He will enter.

2 They will follow.

3 We will encourage.

4 You (pl.) will enter.

5 I will speak.

6 I will try.

7 He will follow.

8 He will set out.

9 They will encourage.

10 They will try.

1 mark for each question. Total: 10

Exercise 14.10

1 You (pl.) will speak.

2 We will try.

3 They will set out.

4 They will speak.

5 He will encourage.

6 You (s.) will speak./You (s.) speak.

7 We will enter.

8 You (s.) will try.

9 We will speak.

10 You (s.) will follow./You (s.) follow.

1 mark for each question. Total: 10

Exercise 14.11

1 You (pl.) will try.

2 You (pl.) will follow.

3 You (pl.) will encourage.

4 They will enter.

5 We will follow.

6 He will try.

7 He will speak.

8 You (s.) will set out./You (s.) set out.

9 I will encourage.

10 I will set out.

1 mark for each question. Total: 10

Exercise 14.12

1 We follow.

2 We will follow.

3 We will enter.

4 They were trying.

5 They were encouraging.

6 We enter.

7 You were trying.

8 They will enter.

9 He follows.

10 He was setting out.

1 mark for each question. Total: 10

Exercise 14.13

1 You (pl.) were entering.

2 You (s.) set out./You (s.) will set out.

3 You (pl.) will try.

4 They set out.

5 They encourage.

6 You (pl.) will encourage.

7 You (pl.) enter.

8 They were entering.

9 He will try.

10 We were speaking.

1 mark for each question. Total: 10

Exercise 14.14

1 I set out.

2 You (s.) were following.

3 You (pl.) speak.

4 You (pl.) will follow.

5 I encourage.

6 I was setting out.

7 You (pl.) follow.

8 He will speak.

9 We speak.

10 I will set out.

1 mark for each question. Total: 10

Exercise 14.15

1 He tried.

2 She tried.

3 He had tried.

4 She had tried.

5 They tried.

6 They had tried.

7 They had followed.

8 She spoke.

9 They had set out.

10 You (pl.) entered.

1 mark for each question. Total: 10

Exercise 14.16

1 You (s.) encouraged.

2 You (pl.) followed.

3 She entered.

4 We spoke.

5 He set out.

6 She set out.

7 He had encouraged.

8 He followed.

9 We set out.

10 They spoke.

1 mark for each question. Total: 10

Exercise 14.17

1 He entered.

2 She had spoken.

3 They set out.

4 He had spoken.

5 You (pl.) had entered.

6 He spoke.

7 You (pl.) had followed.

8 We entered.

9 She had entered.

10 She encouraged.

1 mark for each question. Total: 10

Exercise 14.18

1 A good general always encourages his soldiers. (6)

2 I will try to do this tomorrow. (4)

3 The king spoke many words to the citizens. (6)

4 The slaves entered the villa. (5)

5 The father spoke these words, then he departed. (7)

6 The mother encouraged her son to work well. (7)

7 The slaves tried to escape from the city. (6)

8 That boy was following this girl. (5)

9 The soldiers set out from the captured town. (6)

10 The king encouraged the citizens to defend the city bravely. (8)

Total: 60

Exercise 14.19

1 Menelaus set out to the city of Troy. (6)

2 Many ships followed him. (5)

3 The Greeks tried to capture Troy quickly. (6)

4 The Greeks finally entered the city of Troy. (7)

5 Agamemnon encouraged the Greeks to fight well. (7)

6 The general spoke many words to his friends. (6)

7 The general encouraged his friends to prepare ships. (7)

8 The general and his companions set out from the city of Troy. (8)

9 The Greeks were trying to return home. (4)

10 The Greeks wanted to set out soon. (4)

Total: 60

Exercise 14.20

1 Why are you speaking, boys? Work! (4)

2 Do not speak, boy. Work! (4)

3 The general will encourage the soldiers tomorrow. (4)

4 The slaves were trying to escape into the temple. (5)

5 The master however was following the slaves. (4)

6 We set out from the city yesterday. (5)

7 The ships set out from the harbour quickly. (6)

8 The teacher ordered the pupils not to speak. (5)

9 I know that all girls like to speak. (5)

10 I hear that all the ships have already set out from the harbour. (8)

Total: 50

Exercise 14.21

1 The general persuaded the citizens to follow him. (6)

2 The master ordered the slave to enter the villa. (7)

3 I do not want to follow this general. (4)

4 Do not speak, pupils! Listen to me! (5)

5 This boy never tries to work. (5)

6 Menelaus encouraged the Greeks to set out to the city immediately. (9)

7 The Greeks wanted to set out from the city soon. (6)

8 Dead men never speak. (4)

9 The ships of the Greeks had set out from the harbour without delay. (8)

10 The soldiers soon entered the town. (6)

Total: 60

Exercise 14.22

1 hostes flumen transierunt. (3)

2 milites fortes trans mare navigaverunt. (5)

3 verba sapientia magistri audimus. (4)

4 duces virtutem laudant. (3)

5 tempestas magna multas naves delevit. (5)

Total: 20

Exercise 14.23

1 discipuli sapientes a magistris laudantur. (5)

2 corpus in nave inventum est. (4)

3 dominus a servo forti defendebatur. (5)

4 iuvenis laudabatur. (2)

5 multa praemia militibus data sunt. (4)

Total: 20

Exercise 14.24

1 proficiscimur/profecti/profectae sumus.   3 sequimur.

2 ingredior.   4 hortabar.

5 conamur.

6 sequuntur.

7 ingredieris.

8 proficiscor.

9 loquitur.

10 loquebantur.

1 mark for each question. Total: 10

Exercise 14.25

1 conor.

2 hortabimur.

3 loquebatur.

4 sequemini.

5 proficiscebantur.

6 ingredimur.

7 sequar.

8 sequebantur.

9 loquuntur.

10 hortatur.

1 mark for each question. Total: 10

Exercise 14.26

1 profectus est.

2 profecta est.

3 profecti/profectae/profecta sunt.

4 hortati/hortatae sumus.

5 conatus/conata sum.

6 locuti/locutae/locuta sunt.

7 locuta est.

8 secutus es.

9 ingressus est.

10 hortati/hortatae/hortata estis.

1 mark for each question. Total: 10

Exercise 14.27

1 conati/conatae/conata erant.

2 locutus erat.

3 locuta erat.

4 ingressi/ingressae eramus.

5 profecti/profectae/profecta erant.

6 hortati/hortatae/hortata eratis.

7 secutus/secuta eram.

8 ingressus/ingressa/ingressum eras.

9 conata erat.

10 hortatus erat.

1 mark for each question. Total: 10

Exercise 14.28

1 naves ducis e portu cras proficiscentur.

2 discipuli boni bene laborare semper conantur.

3 milites ex urbe secunda hora profecti sunt.

4 duces boni milites hortari semper volunt.

5 hostes in urbem media nocte subito ingressi sunt.

6 marks for each question. Total: 30

Exercise 14.29

1 dux milites hortabitur ut bene pugnent. (6)

2 nautae e portu statim proficisci volebant. (6)

3 in hanc villam ingredior. noli me sequi! (7)

4 multi viri fortissimi hoc flumen transire conati erant, sed frustra. (10)

5 scimus illum magistrum discipulos semper hortari. (6)

Total: 35

Exercise 14.30

1 conveniremus.

2 vinceremur.

3 superaret.

4 caperemini.

5 pugnaremus.

1 mark for each question. Total: 5

Exercise 14.31

1 nesciebat.	He did not know.
2 conatus/conata/conatum est.	He/she/it tried.
3 loquuntur.	They speak.
4 secutus/secuta sum.	I followed.
5 habitabamus.	We were living.
6 invenietur.	He will be found.
7 legebatur.	He was being chosen/read.
8 scripserunt.	They wrote.
9 feceras.	You had made.
10 ibit.	He will go.

2 marks for each question. Total: 20

Exercise 14.32

1 2nd person	Singular	Present	Indicative	Active	possum
2 1st person	Plural	Future	Indicative	Active	scio
3 3rd person	Singular	Imperfect	Indicative	Passive	do
4 3rd person	Singular	Perfect	Indicative	Active	dico
5 3rd person	Plural	Perfect	Indicative	Active	exeo
6 3rd person	Singular	Imperfect	Subjunctive	Active	fugio

7	1st person	Plural	Future	Indicative	Active	habeo
8	1st person	Plural	Imperfect	Indicative	Active	habito
9	3rd person	Singular	Present	Indicative	Active	navigo
10	1st person	Singular	Pluperfect	Indicative	Active	pono

6 marks for each question. Total: 60

Exercise 14.33

1 mulieres pecunias amant.	Women like money.	(3 + 3)
2 puellae loquuntur.	The girls are speaking.	(2 + 2)
3 senes ambulare conati sunt.	The old men tried to walk.	(3 + 3)
4 matres filias secutae sunt.	The mothers followed their daughters.	(3 + 3)
5 exercitus in urbibus erant.	Armies were in the cities.	(4 + 4)

Total: 30

Exercise 14.34

1 animal saevum effugit.	The savage animal escaped.	(3 + 3)
2 nauta proficiscitur.	The sailor sets out.	(2 + 2)
3 dux militem hortabatur.	The general was encouraging the soldier.	(3 + 3)
4 custos servum secutus est.	The guard followed the slave.	(3 + 3)
5 navis ex insula profecta est.	The ship set out from the island.	(4 + 4)

Total: 30

Exercise 14.35

1 No one is wiser than I.	(5)
2 This is the good slave to whom I gave the food.	(7)
3 We captured the city and destroyed it.	(3)
4 Don't shout! We are trying to work.	(4)
5 That road is longer than this one.	(6)

Total: 25

Exercise 15.1

When the Greeks had stayed on Circe's island for one year,[6] they finally decided to set out[3] in order to return home and see their families again.[7] While they were sailing across the sea[3] they saw many monsters, underwent many dangers [and] suffered many hardships.[9] Finally all the Greeks, except for Ulysses himself, were either killed or dead.[8] Ulysses himself, driven by the waves and winds, finally arrived at the island of Ogygia,[8] where the beautiful nymph Calypso lived.[4] When Calypso had seen Ulysses,[3] she loved him greatly and wanted to marry him.[5] However, since he loved his wife and wanted to return home, he refused.[8] Calypso kept Ulysses on her island for seven years.[6] Finally, ordered by the gods and after a raft had been built,[5] she allowed Ulysses to depart from her island.[5]

Total: 80

Exercise 15.2

1 (a) proficisci/passi sunt/mortui erant.		(1)
(b) interfecti/actus/iussa/facta.		(1)
(c) proficisci/nubere/redire/discedere.		(1)
2 Subjunctive.		(1)
3 Accusative. After the preposition **trans**.		(2)
4 3rd. Singular. Perfect. **nolo**.		(4)

Total: 10

Exercise 15.3

1 When the boys had seen the teacher, they fled.		(5)
2 When the teacher had punished the boy, he laughed.		(5)
3 When the soldiers had killed many men, they captured the city.		(7)
4 When the boys had gone into the villa, they heard mother.		(7)
5 When the Romans had captured the city, they destroyed it.		(6)
6 When the poet had read the book, he was happy.		(6)
7 When the slaves had finished the task, they were happy.		(6)
8 When the soldiers had fought well, they received many rewards.		(7)
9 When the soldiers had seen the enemy, they were afraid.		(5)
10 When the Romans had caught sight of the enemy, they attacked immediately.		(6)

Total: 60

Exercise 15.4

1 When Paris had seen and loved Helen, he captured her immediately. (8)

2 When Paris had taken Helen, Menelaus was angry. (7)

3 When the soldiers had prepared everything, they set out. (6)

4 When the Greeks had prepared great forces, they sailed to the city of Troy. (9)

5 When the Greeks had sailed to the city of Troy, they attacked the walls. (8)

6 When the Greeks had attacked the city for ten years, they finally made a huge horse. (10)

7 When the Greeks had made a huge horse, they left it near the city. (9)

8 When the citizens had caught sight of the horse, they led it into the city. (8)

9 When the citizens had led the horse into the city, they were happy. (8)

10 When the Greeks had destroyed Troy, they returned to Greece. (7)

Total: 80

Exercise 15.5

1 While/When the farmer was working in the fields, he saw many horses. (8)

2 Since the soldiers were tired, they did not fight well. (7)

3 While/When the general was sleeping, he was killed by a slave. (7)

4 Since the soldiers were afraid of the enemy, they did not want to fight. (6)

5 While/When many ships were sailing towards the island, they were destroyed by a storm. (9)

6 Since the master did not like the slave, he killed him. (7)

7 Since the daring soldiers were fighting bravely, they received many wounds. (8)

8 While/When the city was being attacked by the enemy, many citizens escaped. (8)

9 Since the boys did not like the cruel teacher, they did not used to work. (8)

10 Since the boy was not working, the teacher was angry. (7)

Total: 75

Exercise 15.6

1 Since the teacher was angry, he punished the boy. (6)

2 Since the teacher had punished the boy, the boy was sad. (7)

3 Since the boy was sad, he cried. (5)

4 Since the boy was crying, his mother was angry. (7)

5 Since the boy's mother was angry, she hurried to the teacher. (8)

6 Since the boy's mother was angry, the teacher was afraid. (7)

7 Since he was frightened, the teacher fled immediately. (6)

8 Since the teacher had fled, the boys did not work. (6)

9 Since the slave was running quickly, no one was able to capture him. (8)

10 Since the goddess knew that she was not able to kill Ulysses, she was angry. (10)

Total: 70

Chapter 15

Exercise 15.7

1 laborem non amamus. (3)

2 milites multa animalia in silvis interfecerunt/occiderunt/necaverunt. (6)

3 vocem reginae non amabam. (4)

4 parentes crudeles puerum terruerunt. (4)

5 pro patria pugnamus. (3)

Total: 20

Exercise 15.8

1 senex in urbe relictus est. (4)

2 naves tempestate delentur. (3)

3 multa tela a militibus fortibus iacta sunt. (6)

4 pecunia domini a militibus custodiebatur. (5)

5 dei laudantur. (2)

Total: 20

Exercise 15.9

1 nautae, nave parata, profecti sunt. (5)

2 milites, urbe deleta, discesserunt. (5)

3 discipuli, verbis magistri auditis, laeti erant. (7)

4 senex, puella pulchra visa, risit. (6)

5 puellae, cum multas horas cucurrissent, fessae erant. (7)

Total: 30

Exercise 15.10

1 milites, cum fortes essent, bene pugnaverunt. (6)

2 cum navigaremus, multas naves vidimus. (5)

3 dominus, cum crudelis esset, servos puniebat. (6)

4 cum per viam ambularem, puellam pulchram vidi. (7)

5 agricolae, cum laborarent, multa animalia viderunt. (6)

Total: 30

Exercise 15.11

1 fuissem.

2 portati/portatae/portata essent.

3 dedisset.

4 posses.

5 defenderetur.

1 mark for each question. Total: 5

Exercise 15.12

1 3rd person	Singular	Present	Indicative	Passive	**rego**
2 3rd person	Singular	Imperfect	Subjunctive	Active	**timeo**
3 3rd person	Singular	Pluperfect	Subjunctive	Active	**video**
4 3rd person	Singular	Imperfect	Indicative	Passive	**specto**
5 1st person	Plural	Pluperfect	Indicative	Active	**mitto**
6 3rd person	Plural	Perfect	Indicative	Active	**voco**
7 3rd person	Singular	Perfect	Indicative	Active	**trado**
8 3rd person	Singular	Imperfect	Subjunctive	Active	**sto**
9 1st person	Plural	Imperfect	Indicative	Active	**sedeo**
10 3rd person	Singular	Perfect	Indicative	Active	**scribo**

6 marks for each question. Total: 60

Exercise 15.13

1 discesserunt.	They departed.
2 curram.	I will run.
3 poterimus.	We will be able.
4 tuli.	I carried.
5 mortuus/mortua/mortuum est.	He/she/it died.
6 pati.	To suffer.
7 amabamur.	We were being loved.
8 volent.	They will want.
9 ite!	Go!
10 nolebas.	You did not want.

2 marks for each question. Total: 20

Exercise 15.14

1 Why is my father going towards the wall? (6)

2 We all greatly love money. (4)

3 The boys ran out of the fields into the villa. (6)

4 The master killed the slave because he never used to work well. (7)

5 The miserable slave was killed by the cruel master. (7)

Total: 30

Exercise 16.1

When Ulysses set out from the island of Ogygia,(5) he went on for many days on his raft(5) and was finally driven to the island of the Phaeacians,(6) whose king was Alcinous.(4) When Alcinous had given him gold and many gifts,(6) he finally asked him who he was.(5) Ulysses explained that he was Ulysses;(4) that he and his army had captured Troy;(5) that all of his companions had either died or been killed;(6) that he wanted to see his wife and son again.(7)

The Phaeacians, having heard Ulysses' words,(4) encouraged him not to be afraid.(4) They put gifts in his ship and carried Ulysses to the island of Ithaca with magical speed.(8) Ulysses, having got off his ship, was finally standing in his own homeland.(6)

Total: 75

Exercise 16.2

1 (a) quorum.   (1)

(b) dedisset.   (1)

(c) se.   (1)

(d) verbis ... auditis/donis ... positis.   (1)

(e) cepisse/mortuos ... esse/interfectos esse.   (1)

2 Accusative.   Accusative of time 'how long'.   (2)

3 Ablative.   (1)

4 Perfect.   fero.   (2)

Total: 10

Exercise 16.3

1 The tired slave tried to escape and was captured by his master.   (8)

2 The girls set out at dawn and soon arrived at the city.   (8)

3 The daring general encouraged his soldiers and charged into battle.   (8)

4 The boy entered the villa and saw his friend.   (6)

5 The girl entered the villa and saw her friend.   (6)

6 The soldier suffered many wounds and died.   (6)

7 The sailors went on for many days and were finally driven to the island.   (9)

8 The brave soldier died in that battle and was praised by his companions. (10)

9 The slaves went out of the temple and hurried home. (6)

10 The soldiers followed their general for a long time and finally fought against
the enemy. (8)

Total: 75

Exercise 16.4

1 The Greek soldiers set out from Greece and sailed to the city of Troy. (9)

2 Menelaus encouraged all the Greeks and ordered them to prepare ships. (8)

3 The ships of the Greeks went on for many days and finally arrived at the city of Troy. (11)

4 The Greeks tried to capture Troy for many years and decided to build a huge horse on
the beach. (11)

5 The Greeks went out of the horse and killed many Trojans. (7)

6 The citizens suffered many wounds and were killed by the Greeks. (8)

7 The king encouraged the Trojans to collect weapons and charged against the Greeks. (9)

8 The rest of the Greeks entered the city and killed many Trojans. (8)

9 The ships set out from harbour and soon arrived at the city of Troy. (9)

10 Many Trojans died in the battle and were praised by all the citizens. (10)

Total: 90

Exercise 16.5

1 vir, haec verba locutus, discessit. (5)

2 femina/mulier, haec verba locuta, discessit. (5)

3 navis, statim profecta, mox advenit. (5)

4 dux, milites hortatus, progressus est. (4)

5 Romani tamen, bene pugnare conati, victi sunt. (6)

Total: 25

Exercise 16.6

1 regina, multa vulnera passa, mortua est. (5)

2 Romani, hostes trans montes secuti, statim oppugnaverunt. (7)

3 iuvenis, in villam ingressus, multos amicos vidit. (6)

4 dux, ad flumen progressus, milites hortatus est. (6)

5 servi, ex oppido egressi, in agros cucurrerunt. (6)

Total: 30

Chapter 16

Exercise 16.7

1 viri mulieres diu spectabant. The men were looking at the women for a long time. (3 + 4)

2 milites fortes muros oppugnaverunt. The brave soldiers attacked the walls. (4 + 4)

3 pueri illas puellas iam conspexerant. The boys had already caught sight of those girls. (4 + 5)

4 homines mortuos in viis vidimus. We saw dead men in the streets. (4 + 5)

5 naves ad portus pellebantur. Ships were being driven towards the harbours. (3 + 4)

Total: 40

Exercise 16.8

1 donum saepe accipio. I often receive a present. (2 + 3)

2 senex pugnare noluit. The old man did not want to fight. (3 + 3)

3 civis oppidum bene defendebat. The citizen was defending the town well. (3 + 4)

4 miles a servo custodiebatur. The soldier was being guarded by a slave. (3 + 4)

5 scutum a puero saepe ferebatur. A shield was often being carried by the boy. (4 + 6)

Total: 35

Exercise 16.9

1 ivissent/iissent.

2 vocatus/vocata/vocatum esset.

3 mansissem.

4 scriberes.

5 regerentur.

1 mark for each question. Total: 5

Exercise 16.10

1 progreditur. He goes forward.

2 dederunt. They gave.

3 dicebantur. They were being said.

4 exierunt. They went out.

5 potes. You (s.) are able.

6 videramus. We had seen.

7 veniebatis. You (pl.) were coming.

8 iussit. He ordered.

9 movebatur. He was being moved.

10 navigabimus. We will sail.

2 marks for each question. Total: 20

Exercise 16.11

1 1st person	Singular	Perfect	Indicative	Active	**sum**
2 3rd person	Singular	Pluperfect	Subjunctive	Active	**moveo**
3 3rd person	Plural	Imperfect	Indicative	Active	**timeo**
4 2nd person	Singular	Future	Indicative	Active	**eo**
5 3rd person	Singular	Pluperfect	Indicative	Active	**constituo**
6 3rd person	Singular	Pluperfect	Indicative	Active	**pono**
7 3rd person	Plural	Perfect	Indicative	Active	**fero**
8 3rd person	Singular	Pluperfect	Indicative	Passive	**amo**
9 2nd person	Singular	Imperfect	Subjunctive	Active	**sum**
10 1st person	Plural	Imperfect	Indicative	Active	**nolo**

6 marks for each question. Total: 60

Exercise 16.12

1 I am not able to play today. (4)

2 Having done this, all the women departed immediately. (6)

3 A very big horse was made by the Greeks. (6)

4 The name of this girl is Cornelia. (5)

5 That man is famous. His sons are also famous. (9)

Total: 30

Exercise 16.13

1 milites multa arma collegerunt. (4)

2 matrem caram habemus. (3)

3 in media urbe stabas. (4)

4 clamores hostium audivimus. (3)

5 turba magna ad templa deorum currebat. (6)

Total: 20

Exercise 16.14

1 multae viae longae a Romanis aedificatae sunt. (6)

2 pecunia in via a servo felici inventa est. (7)

3 servi puniuntur. (2)

4 Graeci victi sunt. (2)

5 lux clara visa est. (3)

Total: 20

Exercise 17.1

Having captured Troy[2], the chieftains of the Greeks had now returned to their homelands.[5] On the island of Ithaca however, because Penelope, the wife of Ulysses,[6] had not seen her husband for many years,[5] she was so sad that she often used to cry.[6] Many noble men meanwhile had come to Penelope's palace.[5] These men believed that Ulysses was dead;[5] that he would never return home.[3] They thought that Penelope would never see her husband again.[5] They all wanted to marry Penelope, a beautiful and rich woman.[6] Penelope however did not want to choose a new husband.[5] For she hoped that Ulysses would soon arrive at Ithaca,[6] and that then the suitors would depart from her palace.[5] Penelope did not know that Ulysses was already present on the island of Ithaca.[6]

Total: 70

Exercise 17.2

1 (a) Troia capta.   (1)

  (b) fleret.   (1)

  (c) esse/ducere/eligere/adesse.   (1)

2 3rd.   Plural.   Pluperfect.   redeo.   (4)

3 Accusative.   Accusative of time 'how long'.   (2)

4 putare means 'to think' and *reputation* means what people think of you.   (1)

Total: 10

Exercise 17.3

1 The teacher knows that the boy will work.

2 The teacher knows that the boys will work.

3 The teacher knew that the boy would work.

4 The teacher knew that the boys would work.

5 The teacher knows that the girl will work.

6 The teacher knows that the girls will work.

7 The teacher knew that the girl would work.

8 The teacher knew that the girls would work.

9 I know that the danger will be great.

10 I knew that the dangers would be great.

5 marks for each question. Total: 50

Exercise 17.4

1 The teacher knows that this boy will work well. (7)

2 I know that I will never have much money. (7)

3 The man believes that the girl will come soon. (6)

4 The man believed that the girl would come soon. (6)

5 The general says that the war will be long. (6)

6 The general said that the war would be long. (6)

7 The messenger announced that the enemy would arrive soon. (6)

8 Everyone knew that the Greeks would destroy Troy. (6)

9 They know that that slave will not do this. (7)

10 The slave said that in a short time he would kill the master. (8)

Total: 65

Exercise 17.5

1 I know that this pupil will never work. (6)

2 I hope that that girl will come soon. (6)

3 The slaves hope that they will not be punished by the master. (8)

4 The sailors hope that this storm will not be big. (7)

5 The slaves knew that this task would be difficult. (7)

6 The Romans believed that they would soon conquer the Greeks. (7)

7 I do not believe that you will do this. (6)

8 The general believed that he would arrive at the city before night. (9)

9 The pupils hoped that the teacher would not arrive. (6)

10 The master knew that those slaves would not do this. (8)

Total: 70

Exercise 17.6

1 Menelaus said that he would collect great forces. (7)

2 Menelaus said that he would destroy the city of Troy. (7)

3 The Greeks said that they would send help to Menelaus. (8)

4 Menelaus knew that many soldiers and many ships would arrive soon. (9)

5 Menelaus said that he would send an army against the Trojans. (8)

6 Menelaus said that an army would be sent against the Trojans. (7)

Chapter 17

7 The Greeks said that they would punish the Trojans. (6)

8 The Greeks said that they would soon capture the city of Troy. (8)

9 The Greeks knew that the Trojans would defend the city bravely. (7)

10 The Trojans believed that they would never be overcome by the Greeks. (8)

Total: 75

Exercise 17.7

1 The Greeks knew that the Trojan citizens would fight bravely. (7)

2 The Greeks believed that this war would be long. (7)

3 The Trojans knew that they would finally be beaten by the Greeks. (8)

4 The Trojans did not know that the Greeks would build a huge horse. (7)

5 The Trojans said that they would lead the horse into the city. (8)

6 Aeolus said that he would give a bag of winds to Ulysses. (8)

7 Ulysses did not know that his companions would do this. (7)

8 Penelope knew that she would not see her husband for a long time. (9)

9 Penelope hoped that Ulysses would return home soon. (7)

10 The suitors hoped that Penelope would choose a new husband. (7)

Total: 75

Exercise 17.8

1 Penelope sperat Ulixem domum mox rediturum esse. (6)

2 putabam hunc discipulum bene et diu laboraturum esse. (7)

3 credimus naves cras adventuras esse. (4)

4 scis milites bene pugnaturos esse. (4)

5 sciebas milites bene pugnaturos esse. (4)

Total: 25

Exercise 17.9

1 dux sciebat hunc militem audacem futurum esse/fore. (6)

2 audimus magistrum librum longum scripturum esse. (5)

3 cives sciebant hostes muros urbis oppugnaturos esse. (6)

4 Ulixes nesciebat comites hoc facturos esse. (5)

5 ille magister putat omnes puellas semper bene laboraturas esse. (8)

Total: 30

Exercise 17.10

1	3rd person	Singular	Imperfect	Subjunctive	Active	**eligo**
2	3rd person	Plural	Imperfect	Subjunctive	Active	**spero**
3	2nd person	Singular	Imperfect	Subjunctive	Active	**possum**
4	3rd person	Plural	Imperfect	Subjunctive	Active	**curro**
5	2nd person	Plural	Pluperfect	Subjunctive	Active	**curro**
6	3rd person	Singular	Pluperfect	Subjunctive	Deponent	**progredior**
7	3rd person	Plural	Imperfect	Subjunctive	Active	**scio**
8	3rd person	Singular	Pluperfect	Subjunctive	Active	**eo**
9	1st person	Singular	Imperfect	Subjunctive	Active	**persuadeo**
10	2nd person	Singular	Pluperfect	Subjunctive	Active	**possum**

6 marks for each question. Total: 60

Exercise 17.11

1	putabam.	I was thinking.
2	elegerunt.	They chose.
3	sperabis.	You (s.) will hope.
4	progressi/progressae/ progressa erant.	They had gone forward.
5	sciebamus.	We knew.
6	moriemur.	We will die.
7	iuverant.	They had helped.
8	imperavit.	He ordered.
9	persuaserat.	He had persuaded.
10	coacti/coactae/coacta estis.	You (pl.) were forced.

2 marks for each question. Total: 20

Exercise 17.12

1 Having seen these men, I was afraid.	(3)
2 When I entered the city, I saw many bodies.	(6)
3 We are running quickly.	(2)
4 The boy was following the girl because he loved her.	(6)
5 Because the young man had drunk much wine, he was not able to walk.	(8)

Total: 25

Exercise 18.1

Ulysses, carried to the island of Ithaca with the help of the Phaeacians,(4) was so tired that he was sleeping on the beach.(4) The goddess Athena finally woke him up and spoke these words to him:(6) 'Get up, Ulysses!(2) I do not know why you are sleeping.(3) Don't stay near the beach!(3) You must go forward to the palace(3) in order to find out what is being done there.(5) Many suitors are present.(3) They are drinking your wine.(3) They are eating your food.(3) They want to marry your wife Penelope in order to gain your wealth.(5) I will change you into a beggar so that you can find out everything secretly.(7) In this way you will not be recognised.(3) No one will know who you really are.'(4) Having said these words,(2) the goddess changed Ulysses into a beggar.(4) He set out from the beach and soon arrived at his own palace.(6)

Total: 70

Exercise 18.2

1 (a) progredi/locuta est/profectus.	(1)
(b) dormiret.	(1)
(c) ego/te.	(1)
2 fero. I carry.	(2)
3 velle.	(1)
4 Accusative. Object of the verb.	(2)
5 Future. Passive.	(2)

Total: 10

Exercise 18.3

1 Let us enter!

2 Let us not laugh!

3 Let them stay!

4 Let us go!

5 Let us depart!

6 Let us sail!

7 Let us run!

8 Let me sleep!

9 Let them be punished!

10 Let me be heard!

2 marks for each question. Total: 20

Exercise 18.4

1 Let him not be killed, o soldier!	(3)
2 Let us work well, o Romans!	(3)

3 Let us not be overcome by the Romans! (4)

4 Let us attack the town! (2)

5 Let wine be drunk now! (3)

6 Let the slaves be punished! (2)

7 Let the king rule well! (3)

8 Let the pupils work well! (3)

9 Let us throw our javelins! (3)

10 Let the soldiers be praised by the general! (4)

Total: 30

Exercise 18.5

1 May all lands be ruled well by the Romans! (6)

2 Let us defend the city well! (3)

3 Let us drink much wine! (3)

4 Let us not be afraid of the enemy! (3)

5 Let us escape quickly! (2)

6 Let us not be caught sight of by the teacher! (4)

7 Let us be brave and daring! (4)

8 Let us praise the teacher! (2)

9 Let us lead the horse into the city! (4)

10 Let us not be conquered by the enemy! (4)

Total: 35

Exercise 18.6

1 The pupils are working well in order to be wise. (6)

2 I am running in order to arrive home quickly. (5)

3 The chieftains are returning to Greece in order to see their wives again. (8)

4 The Greeks are building a huge horse in order to capture Troy. (8)

5 This slave is running quickly in order not to be caught sight of by the master. (8)

6 The citizens are fighting bravely in order to defend the city. (6)

7 The Trojan citizens are fighting well in order not to be captured by the Greeks. (7)

8 I want to run quickly in order to be able to escape from danger. (8)

9 The enemy are coming to kill us! (5)

10 This pupil always works well in order not to be punished by the master. (9)

Total: 70

Exercise 18.7

1 I am warning you to do this immediately. (6)

2 I am warning you not to do this again. (6)

3 The teacher always warns the boys to work. (6)

4 I am warning you not to be bad. (5)

5 I will warn my daughter not to play in the road. (6)

6 I order you to work. (4)

7 I am warning the boy to go home. (5)

8 This teacher will never persuade me to work. (7)

9 A wise general always encourages soldiers to fight well. (8)

10 The general orders the sailors to sail to Italy. (7)

Total: 60

Exercise 18.8

1 surgamus! (1)

2 festinemus! (1)

3 ne vincamur! (2)

4 progrediamur! (1)

5 hodie constituat! (2)

6 flumen ibi transeamus! (3)

7 urbem oppugnent! (2)

8 puellas hic exspectemus! (3)

9 ne magistrum audiamus! (3)

10 patrem rogemus! (2)

Total: 20

Exercise 18.9

1 magister puellae imperat ut laboret.

2 patri persuadebo ut pecuniam mihi det.

3 milites hortabimur ut oppidum oppugnent.

4 dominus servis imperat ne loquantur.

5 te/vos moneo ne hoc facias/faciatis.

5 marks for each question. Total: 25

Exercise 18.10

1 festino ut puellam prope portum videam. (6)

2 pugnamus ut urbem nostram defendamus. (5)

3 ad portum it ut navem exspectet. (6)

4 navis discedit ut ad insulam naviget. (6)

5 milites arma sua colligunt ut contra hostes pugnent. (7)

Total: 30

Exercise 18.11

1 What ought I to do now? (4)

2 You (s.) ought to hurry home. (3)

3 You (s.) ought to do this soon. (4)

4 You ought to get up immediately, boy! (4)

5 I ought to read this book. (4)

6 Small girls never ought to cry. (5)

7 We will have to fight well, soldiers! (4)

8 Good pupils ought to listen to their teachers. (5)

9 You (pl.) ought to listen to the teacher, boys! (4)

10 Small boys ought not to stand in the middle of the road. (8)

Total: 45

Exercise 18.12

1 Good soldiers ought to fight well. (5)

2 We ought to receive many rewards. (4)

3 The ships ought to set out soon. (4)

4 Young men ought not to drink wine. (5)

5 Soldiers always ought to carry swords and shields. (7)

6 Teachers always ought to praise good pupils. (6)

7 Good pupils always ought to be praised by their teachers. (7)

8 Your slave ought to work well. (5)

9 We will have to be brave in this battle, companions! (7)

10 I must depart from the city now. (5)

Total: 55

Exercise 18.13

1 festinare debeo. (2)

2 nuntius currere debet. (3)

3 laborare debes. (2)

4 reges regere debent. (3)

5 clamare non debetis. (2)

6 cives bene laborare debebunt. (4)

7 hanc urbem capere debemus. (4)

8 statim discedere debeo. (3)

9 quid facere debemus? (3)

10 nunc librum scribere debemus. (4)

Total: 30

Exercise 18.14

1	3rd person	Singular	Present	Subjunctive	Active	**sum**
2	3rd person	Singular	Imperfect	Subjunctive	Active	**sum**
3	3rd person	Singular	Pluperfect	Subjunctive	Active	**sum**
4	3rd person	Plural	Imperfect	Subjunctive	Active	**sum**
5	3rd person	Plural	Imperfect	Subjunctive	Passive	**video**
6	3rd person	Plural	Imperfect	Subjunctive	Active	**eo**
7	2nd person	Singular	Pluperfect	Subjunctive	Active	**surgo**
8	1st person	Plural	Present	Subjunctive	Passive	**vinco**
9	1st person	Plural	Present	Subjunctive	Active	**volo**
10	3rd person	Singular	Pluperfect	Subjunctive	Active	**cognosco**

6 marks for each question. Total: 60

Exercise 18.15

1 That king was not liked by all the citizens. (7)

2 Not all the citizens liked the king. (5)

3 The general ordered the soldiers to advance to the river immediately. (7)

4 That old man is wise. He knows many things. (6)

5 We will all go into the city tomorrow. (5)

Total: 30

Exercise 19.1

Penelope, Ulysses' wife, and Telemachus, Ulysses' son, were in the palace.(9) The suitors were also present there:(4) they were drinking wine and eating food.(5) Many of them had drunk so much wine that they were drunk.(8) When Telemachus had seen the drunken suitors he was so angry that he decided to tell them off.(10) He went up to them and said these words:(5) 'Noblemen, you are always present here;(4) you are always eating our food.(4) Now you have drunk so much wine that you are drunk.(7) I know why you are present here.(4) My mother however does not believe that Ulysses is dead.(7) She knows that he will soon be present here.(4) Why do you stay in our palace?(4) You are very wicked!(2) Depart from here!'(2) The suitors however did not reply to Telemachus.(4) They were so drunk that they were not listening to what Ulysses' son was saying.(7)

Total: 90

Exercise 19.2

1 (a) regia/procis.		(1)
(b) essent/audirent/diceret.		(1)
(c) progressus.		(1)
2 3rd. Plural. Pluperfect.		(3)
3 is.		(1)
4 mortuum means 'dead' and a *mortuary* is a place for storing dead bodies.		(1)
5 malus. peior.		(2)

Total: 10

Exercise 19.3

1 I am so arrogant that no one likes me.	(7)
2 The boy was so bad that no one liked him.	(8)
3 So many javelins were thrown by the enemy that many were wounded.	(10)
4 The soldiers had made such a long journey that they were tired.	(8)
5 This wine is so good that I often drink it.	(9)
6 The teacher was so cruel that he was feared by everyone.	(8)
7 The boy was so tired that he slept well.	(7)
8 The messenger ran so quickly that he arrived at the city before night.	(10)

9 The battle was so savage that many soldiers died. (9)

10 The teacher was so good that he was liked by all the pupils. (9)

Total: 85

Exercise 19.4

1 That woman was so sad that she was crying. (7)

2 The soldiers were so afraid that they fled. (5)

3 I work so well that I am often praised by the teacher. (8)

4 That master is so cruel that all the slaves are afraid of him. (10)

5 That master was so cruel that all the slaves were afraid of him. (10)

6 The Greeks were so afraid that they ran to the ships quickly. (8)

7 The Greeks were in such great danger that they decided to escape. (8)

8 This boy is so good that the teacher often praises him. (10)

9 That girl was so beautiful that everyone loved her. (9)

10 That slave was working so well that the master gave him money. (10)

Total: 85

Exercise 19.5

1 The Romans fought so well that the enemy were not able to capture the city. (10)

2 The ships were so quick that the Greeks were able to escape. (8)

3 The storm was so savage that it destroyed all the ships. (8)

4 The storm was so savage that all the ships were destroyed. (9)

5 The Romans were so daring that they soon captured the town. (8)

6 This task is so difficult that I am not able to do it. (10)

7 The Romans were so brave that they quickly overcame the enemy. (8)

8 There were so many enemy that we were afraid. (5)

9 There were so many people in the street that we were not able to run. (9)

10 The Romans had built the walls in such a way that the enemy were not able to destroy them. (10)

Total: 85

Exercise 19.6

1 That soldier received so many wounds that finally he was not able to walk. (10)

2 The slave was so frightened of the savage master that he decided to escape. (8)

3 There were so many enemies that we were conquered. (6)

4 He had been wounded to such an extent that he was not able to run. (7)

5 The pupils are so tired that they are always sleeping. (7)

6 That old man speaks so often that no one listens to him. (8)

7 That woman is so beautiful that she is loved by many men. (10)

8 The winds were so strong that they drove the ship to the island quickly. (10)

9 The winds were so strong that the ship was driven to the island quickly. (11)

10 He had such a big shield that he suffered no wound. (8)

Total: 85

Exercise 19.7

1 There were so many enemy that the Romans were afraid. (6 + 1)
  Consecutive/Result clause.

2 I heard that many soldiers had been killed. (5 + 1)
  Indirect statement.

3 I am warning you not to do this. (5 + 1)
  Indirect command.

4 The boy said that he loved that girl. (6 + 1)
  Indirect statement.

5 Boys ought to read books in order to be wise. (7 + 1)
  Final/Purpose clause.

6 So many arrows were fired that we were not able to see the sky. (9 + 1)
  Consecutive/Result clause.

7 The father encouraged his sons not to drink wine. (7 + 1)
  Indirect command.

8 The king said that the Romans had prepared a great army. (6 + 1)
  Indirect statement.

9 The king however ordered the soldiers to set the slaves free. (7 + 1)
  Indirect command.

10 My friend thinks that the city will be captured soon. (7 + 1)
  Indirect statement.

Total: 75

Exercise 19.8

1 3rd person	Singular	Imperfect	Passive	ago
2 1st person	Plural	Present	Active	cognosco
3 3rd person	Plural	Imperfect	Active	audio
4 1st person	Singular	Perfect	Active	facio
5 3rd person	Singular	Perfect	Deponent	morior

6	3rd person	Singular	Perfect	Active	**sum**
7	1st person	Plural	Imperfect	Active	**debeo**
8	3rd person	Singular	Pluperfect	Passive	**cogo**
9	2nd person	Singular	Perfect	Passive	**ago**
10	1st person	Plural	Present	Passive	**capio**

5 marks for each question. Total: 50

Exercise 19.9

1	tam bene laboro ut magister meus me semper laudet.	(9)
2	tot homines in urbe erant ut reginam videre non possemus.	(9)
3	totiens pugnat ut periculum numquam timeat.	(8)
4	puella tam fessa erat ut dormire vellet.	(7)
5	periculum illo die tantum erat ut timeremus.	(7)

Total: 40

Exercise 19.10

1	hic liber tam longus est ut eum legere non possim.	(9)
2	ille magister tam crudelis erat ut omnes eum timerent.	(9)
3	illud opus tam difficile erat ut nemo id facere posset.	(10)
4	regina tam pulchra erat ut ab omnibus amaretur.	(8)
5	totiens in oppido loquor ut nemo me audiat.	(9)

Total: 45

Exercise 19.11

1	Many citizens are going to town today.	(6)
2	We said these words and finally departed.	(5)
3	The general shouted in a loud voice.	(4)
4	A wound had been received by that soldier.	(6)
5	The enemy captured the town and destroyed it.	(4)

Total: 25

Exercise 20.1

While Telemachus was speaking these words to the suitors[6] Penelope noticed an old beggar standing near the doorway.[7] She did not know that this beggar was her husband.[6] She persuaded him to enter.[4] Then, when she had ordered the suitors to give food to the beggar,[7] she asked him who he was, where he had come from, what he wanted [and] where he was going.[10] The beggar replied that he had once been rich[6] but, having suffered many misfortunes, was now poor.[7] He said that he wanted to stay in the palace for a few days[8] and ask for food from the suitors.[5] Penelope, having heard the beggar's words, said:[5] 'Stay with us, beggar.[3] I will order my son to look after you,[5] [and] the suitors to give you food.'[5] Having spoken these words she departed to her bedroom.[6]

Total: 90

Exercise 20.2

1 (a) imperavisset/venisset. (1)

   (b) fuisse. (1)

   (c) se. (1)

   (d) curet/dent. (1)

2 Deponent. (1)

3 Accusative masculine singular of the present participle. (1)

4 imperavisset comes from the verb impero, I order, and *imperial* means connected with an empire – where the emperor gives the orders. (2)

5 Subjunctive.　　Indirect command. (2)

6 volo. (1)

Total: 10

Exercise 20.3

1 I do not know who you (s.) are. (3)

2 I know where he lives. (3)

3 I knew where he lived. (3)

4 I captured the boy and asked him what he was doing. (5)

5 I captured the boys and asked them what they were doing. (5)

6 I do not know why you (s.) are hurrying. (3)

7 I do not know why you (s.) did this. (4)

8 I asked him where he was living. (4)

9 That teacher does not know what he is doing. (5)

10 That teacher did not know what he was doing. (5)

Total: 40

Exercise 20.4

1 The father asks his son why he drinks wine. (6)

2 The father asks his son why he drank wine. (6)

3 The father asked his son what he was drinking. (5)

4 The father asked his son what he had drunk. (5)

5 I do not know what he did. (3)

6 I do not know who is coming. (3)

7 I do not know who came. (3)

8 I did not know who was coming. (3)

9 I did not know who had come. (3)

10 We knew why they were hurrying. (3)

Total: 40

Exercise 20.5

1 Who of you knows where this boy lives? (7)

2 I asked the boy what he was doing here. (5)

3 I asked the boy what he had done. (4)

4 I do not know why this boy is so tired. (7)

5 The messenger announced where the enemy were. (5)

6 The mother did not know where her daughter was. (5)

7 The teacher asked the pupils why they were laughing. (5)

8 The teacher asks the pupils why they are not working. (6)

9 The teacher asked the pupils why they were not working. (6)

10 The boy asked the girl why she was crying. (5)

Total: 55

Exercise 20.6

1 The man asked the master why he had punished the slave. (6)

2 The Romans did not know why the city was being attacked by the enemy. (7)

3 The Romans did not know why the enemy had attacked the city. (6)

4 The farmer asked the slave whether he had seen horses in the fields. (8)

5 The general wanted to find out where the enemy were. (6)

6 The general asked the soldiers why they had come and what they wanted. (8)

7 The teacher did not know whether the girl was laughing or not. (6)

8 I do not know whether these boys are working or playing. (7)

9 We do not know why the slave said these words. (6)

10 We finally found out what the enemy were doing. (5)

Total: 65

Exercise 20.7

1 The Trojans did not know why the Greeks had put a huge horse on the beach. (9)

2 The Trojans did not know why a huge horse had been put on the beach by the Greeks. (11)

3 The Trojans did not know why a huge horse was standing on the beach. (8)

4 The Trojans did not know why the Greeks had departed then. (6)

5 The Trojans did not know whether Greek soldiers were in the horse. (8)

6 The Trojans did not know whether they ought to destroy or receive the horse. (8)

7 The Trojans did not know whether they ought to lead the horse into the city or not. (9)

8 The Trojans did not know what they ought to do. (5)

9 The Greeks did not know what the Trojans would do. (6)

10 The Greeks did not know whether the Trojans would lead the horse into the city or not. (10)

Total: 80

Exercise 20.8

1 No one knew who the beggar was. (5)

2 Penelope asked the beggar where he had come from. (5)

3 Penelope asked him why he was in the palace. (7)

4 Penelope asked him what he wanted. (5)

5 Penelope asked him where he was going. (5)

6 Penelope asked him why he was poor. (6)

7 Penelope asked him whether he was happy or not. (7)

8 Telemachus asked the suitors why they were always drinking wine. (7)

9 The beggar wanted to find out whether Telemachus was brave or not. (8)

10 Telemachus did not know what he ought to do. (5)

Total: 60

Exercise 20.9

1 I know where Marcus lives.   (4 + 1)
Indirect question.

2 I do not know who you (s.) are.   (3 + 1)
Indirect question.

3 The messenger said that he was carrying a book.   (5 + 1)
Indirect statement.

4 The teacher was so stupid that no one used to listen to him.   (8 + 1)
Consecutive/Result clause.

5 The girl was so afraid that she was crying.   (5 + 1)
Consecutive/Result clause.

6 I will go to the city in order to see the queen.   (5 + 1)
Final/Purpose clause.

7 The Romans heard that the enemy were approaching.   (4 + 1)
Indirect statement.

8 He said that he would come soon.   (5 + 1)
Indirect statement.

9 I am running quickly in order not to be captured by the teacher.   (6 + 1)
Final/Purpose clause.

10 I hear that this boy is very stupid.   (5 + 1)
Indirect statement.

Total: 60

Exercise 20.10

1	1st person	Singular	Pluperfect	Active	animadverto
2	1st person	Plural	Present	Active	muto
3	3rd person	Plural	Imperfect	Passive	fero
4	1st person	Plural	Imperfect	Active	nolo
5	1st person	Plural	Present	Active	credo
6	1st person	Singular	Perfect	Passive	fero
7	3rd person	Plural	Imperfect	Active	curo
8	3rd person	Singular	Imperfect	Deponent	sequor
9	1st person	Plural	Present	Passive	pello
10	3rd person	Plural	Imperfect	Passive	interficio

5 marks for each question. Total: 50

Exercise 20.11

1 scio quis/qui sis/sitis.

2 scimus ubi habites/habitetis.

3 nescio cur fleas/fleatis.

4 scit quo eamus.

5 sciunt unde veneris/veneritis.

3 marks for each question. Total: 15

Exercise 20.12

1 post proelium milites nesciebant quid facere deberent. (6)

2 dux milites rogavit cur non pugnarent. (6)

3 dux milites rogavit cur urbem non oppugnavissent. (7)

4 dux milites rogavit num timerent. (5)

5 puellam rogavi utrum rideret an fleret. (6)

Total: 30

Exercise 20.13

1 The general ordered the soldiers to be daring and brave. (7)

2 More daring sailors like faster ships. (5)

3 Where does Marcus live? We do not know. (4)

4 The horses were driven out of the field by the farmer. (7)

5 Many villas were destroyed in that war. (7)

Total: 30

Exercise 21.1

When Ulysses saw the arrogance of the suitors[4] he became so angry that he decided to kill all the suitors.[7] However, fearing that he would not be able to do this alone,[7] he decided to ask the goddess Athena for help[4] and to tell Telemachus that he was really his father Ulysses.[6]

Meanwhile Penelope, who had decided to choose a new husband,[6] called together the suitors and spoke these words to them:[6] 'My Ulysses has been away for many years.[4] I am afraid that I may never see him again.[5] Therefore the man who is able to take Ulysses' bow[7] and shoot an arrow through twelve axes will be my husband.'[9] Having heard these words, the suitors looked at each other.[5] They were worried.[2] They were afraid that they would not be able to do this.[6] Antinous however thought that he was the best of the suitors;[7] he believed that he could do this.[5]

Total: 90

Exercise 21.2

1 (a) constituerit. (1)

  (b) locuta est. (1)

  (c) quae/qui. (1)

2 Accusative.   Accusative of time 'how long'. (2)

3 3rd.   Singular.   Present.   **absum**. (4)

4 bonus. (1)

Total: 10

Exercise 21.3

1 I am afraid that I am not able to do this. (6)

2 The messenger was afraid that the general did/would not believe him. (7)

3 Fearing that the citizens would fight for a long time, the general decided to attack the town immediately. (10)

4 Fearing that they would be punished by their master, the slaves escaped. (7)

5 All the pupils are afraid that the teacher will arrive soon. (7)

6 Fearing that his friend was being/would be killed, the soldier fought bravely. (7)

7 We were afraid that all the ships had been destroyed. (6)

8 I was afraid that my brother was being/would be punished by father. (7)

9 The master is afraid that the slaves may try to escape. (6)

10 The citizens were afraid that the enemy would attack the city soon. (7)

Total: 70

Exercise 21.4

1 The slaves were afraid that they would be killed by the master. (6)

2 The mother was afraid that her son had died in that battle. (9)

3 The master was very afraid that he had killed the slave. (6)

4 The boy is afraid that he did not do this task. (7)

5 The soldiers were afraid that they would be captured by the enemy. (6)

6 The sailor was afraid that the ship was being/would be destroyed by the storm. (6)

7 The sailor was afraid that the storm was destroying/would destroy the ship. (6)

8 The pupils were afraid that they would be punished by the teacher. (6)

9 Fearing that their husbands would perish in the war, their wives asked them not to go. (11)

10 I am afraid that the enemy are preparing great forces today. (7)

Total: 70

Exercise 21.5

1 Menelaus was afraid that Helen had been led to the city of Troy by Paris. (11)

2 The Greeks were afraid that they would not capture Troy quickly. (7)

3 Fearing that Troy would never be captured, the Greeks made a huge horse. (9)

4 Ulysses was afraid that he would never return home. (6)

5 Fearing that her husband would not return, Penelope often used to cry. (8)

6 The Greeks were afraid that they would be killed by Polyphemus. (6)

7 Ulysses was afraid that he himself would not be able to kill all the suitors alone. (10)

8 Penelope was afraid that she would never see her husband again. (7)

9 Penelope was afraid that her husband had been killed in the war. (8)

10 The Trojan citizens were afraid that the city was being/would be captured by the Greeks. (8)

Total: 80

Exercise 21.6

1 magnopere timeo ne interficiamur/occidamur/necemur. (4)

2 timebam ne ille senex hoc faceret. (6)

3 puer timebat ne mater sollicita esset. (6)

Chapter 21

4 omnes nautae timebant ne tempestates navem delerent. (7)

5 servus timebat ne dominus se clamantem audivisset. (7)

Total: 30

Exercise 21.7

1 veritus ne punirer, fugi. (4)

2 veriti ne magister iratus esset, discipuli nihil dixerunt. (6)

3 verita ne mater se vidisset, puella cucurrit. (7)

4 veriti ne urbs caperetur, milites fortiter pugnaverunt. (7)

5 veritae ne viri interfecti/occisi/necati essent, mulieres/feminae flebant. (6)

Total: 30

Exercise 21.8

1 The general found out what the enemy were preparing. (5 + 1)
Indirect question.

2 The general found out what was being prepared by the enemy. (6 + 1)
Indirect question.

3 Our camp is so big that the enemy are not able to capture it. (10 + 1)
Consecutive/Result clause.

4 The soldiers knew that they would be conquered by the enemy. (7 + 1)
Indirect statement.

5 The enemy were running in order not to be killed by the Romans. (6 + 1)
Final/Purpose clause.

6 I do not know why the women are hurrying. (4 + 1)
Indirect question.

7 The sailors entered the city in order to buy food. (6 + 1)
Final/Purpose clause.

8 I asked my friend why the sailors had entered the city. (6 + 1)
Indirect question.

9 The friend replied that the sailors wanted to buy food. (6 + 1)
Indirect statement.

10 I asked him what he was doing. (4 + 1)
Indirect question.

Total: 70

1 The enemy advanced quickly in order to attack the Romans. (7)

2 The boy used to praise himself so much that no one liked him. (8)

3 The man said to his friend that he would give him money. (7)

4 The general said that his soldiers were very brave. (6)

5 You (s.) will never persuade me to do this. (6)

6 He hurried to the city in order to help his friend. (6)

7 We did not know where we were. (3)

8 The master ordered the slaves to hand over the money. (6)

9 The soldiers saw that the enemy were defending the city well. (6)

10 We asked the poet why he had written these words. (5)

Total: 60

Exercise 21.10

1 1st person	Plural	Present	Active	**possum**
2 3rd person	Singular	Imperfect	Active	**sum**
3 3rd person	Plural	Perfect	Active	**servo**
4 3rd person	Singular	Pluperfect	Active	**convoco**
5 1st person	Plural	Imperfect	Active	**effugio**
6 3rd person	Singular	Imperfect	Active	**relinquo**
7 3rd person	Singular	Present	Active	**fio**
8 3rd person	Plural	Imperfect	Passive	**reduco**
9 3rd person	Singular	Pluperfect	Active	**eo**
10 1st person	Plural	Perfect	Passive	**vinco**

5 marks for each question. Total: 50

Exercise 21.11

1 Do not be afraid, friend – I will help you. (6)

2 The master went out of the villa. His slaves followed quickly. (10)

3 We were afraid because a big crowd of farmers was approaching. (6)

4 The soldiers of this king were very brave. (5)

5 Many wise words are often said by that teacher. (8)

Total: 35

Exercise 22.1

When the beggar told him that he was really Ulysses,[5] Telemachus was so happy that he began to cry.[6] Ulysses however ordered him to collect the suitors' weapons and hide them.[7]

Meanwhile in the middle of the palace twelve axes and Ulysses' old bow had been prepared by Penelope's slaves.[12] The suitors were now anxiously looking at the bow and the axes.[6] They were afraid that they would not be able to bend the bow.[5] Antinous took the bow first, but was not able to bend it.[7] Then the beggar asked that the bow be handed over to him.[5] The suitors laughed,[2] fearing that he would be able to bend the bow,[4] but finally, ordered by Telemachus, they handed the bow over to the beggar.[7] He bent the bow without difficulty and fired an arrow.[7] The arrow flew through all the axes.[5] There was silence.[2]

Total: 80

Exercise 22.2

1 (a) inceperit.		(1)
(b) collecta/parati/iussi.		(1)
(c) se/sibi.		(1)
2 Subjunctive.	Indirect command.	(2)
3 Dative.		(1)
4 3rd. Plural. Perfect. trado.		(4)

Total: 10

Exercise 22.3

1	3rd person	Plural	Present	Passive	amo
2	3rd person	Plural	Present	Active	rego
3	1st person	Plural	Present	Active	nolo
4	3rd person	Singular	Imperfect	Active	venio
5	3rd person	Singular	Pluperfect	Active	video
6	3rd person	Plural	Imperfect	Passive	audio
7	3rd person	Plural	Pluperfect	Passive	moneo
8	3rd person	Singular	Present	Active	sum
9	3rd person	Singular	Perfect	Active	curro
10	3rd person	Singular	Perfect	Passive	deleo

5 marks for each question. Total: 50

Exercise 22.4

1 3rd person	Singular	Imperfect	Active	puto
2 1st person	Plural	Imperfect	Active	sum
3 3rd person	Singular	Perfect	Active	cognosco
4 1st person	Plural	Present	Active	eo
5 3rd person	Singular	Present	Passive	curo
6 3rd person	Singular	Imperfect	Active	transeo
7 3rd person	Singular	Pluperfect	Active	convoco
8 1st person	Singular	Present	Active	debeo
9 1st person	Singular	Pluperfect	Active	surgo
10 2nd person	Singular	Perfect	Active	scribo

5 marks for each question. Total: 50

Exercise 22.5

1 2nd person	Plural	Imperfect	Active	discedo
2 3rd person	Singular	Perfect	Passive	occido
3 1st person	Plural	Imperfect	Passive	capio
4 1st person	Singular	Perfect	Active	sum
5 2nd person	Singular	Pluperfect	Active	mitto
6 3rd person	Singular	Imperfect	Active	nolo
7 1st person	Plural	Present	Passive	pello
8 1st person	Singular	Pluperfect	Active	maneo
9 3rd person	Plural	Present	Active	dormio
10 3rd person	Plural	Imperfect	Active	eo

5 marks for each question. Total: 50

Exercise 22.6

1 esset.

2 audiret.

3 conspiceret.

4 duceret.

5 iret.

6 occideret.

7 ambularet.

8 vellet.

9 videret.

10 curreret.

1 mark for each question. Total: 10

Exercise 22.7

1 vincerentur.

2 caperentur.

3 vulnerarentur.

4 punirentur.

5 audirentur.

6 occiderentur.

7 oppugnarentur.

8 liberarentur.

9 interficerentur.

10 viderentur.

1 mark for each question. Total: 10

Exercise 22.8

1 The soldiers found out where the forces of the enemy were.   (6 + 1)
   Indirect question.

2 So many Romans were wounded that they were conquered by the Greeks.   (9 + 1)
   Consecutive/Result clause.

3 The Greeks believed that they would conquer the Romans.   (6 + 1)
   Indirect statement.

4 I asked the boy whether he was laughing or crying.   (6 + 1)
   Indirect question.

5 The general ordered the soldiers not to be afraid.   (5 + 1)
   Indirect command.

6 This wall is so high that we are not able to destroy it.   (10 + 1)
   Consecutive/Result clause.

7 The general asked the soldiers whether they had seen the enemy.   (6 + 1)
   Indirect question.

8 He said that he had seen the queen of the enemy.   (5 + 1)
   Indirect statement.

9 We all knew what the Romans wanted.   (5 + 1)
   Indirect question.

10 The Trojans were afraid that Troy would be captured by the Greeks.   (7 + 1)
   Fear clause.

Total: 75

Exercise 22.9

1 The teacher asked the boys why they were not working.   (6 + 1)
   Indirect question.

2 I hear that this teacher is very bad.   (5 + 1)
   Indirect statement.

3 Mother asked her daughter what she was doing.   (5 + 1)
   Indirect question.

4 The soldiers were so happy that they were shouting in loud voices.   (8 + 1)
   Consecutive/Result clause.

5 The soldier was so afraid of the enemy that he did not want to fight.   (7 + 1)
   Consecutive/Result clause.

6 The soldier shouted that he did not want to fight. (5 + 1)
Indirect statement.

7 The soldier was afraid that he would be killed by the enemy. (6 + 1)
Fear clause.

8 The general ordered the soldier to fight. (6 + 1)
Indirect command.

9 The soldier replied that he would never fight. (6 + 1)
Indirect statement.

10 The general asked the soldier why he had said this. (6 + 1)
Indirect question.

Total: 70

Exercise 22.10

1 The general said that he had come in order to encourage the soldiers. (7 + 2)
Indirect statement. Final/Purpose clause.

2 The general encouraged the soldiers to be brave in order not to be conquered by the enemy. (11 + 2)
Indirect command. Final/Purpose clause.

3 The messengers came to the city in order to find out what the enemy were preparing. (9 + 2)
Final/Purpose clause. Indirect question.

4 The teacher was so amazed that he asked the pupil why he had done this. (10 + 2)
Consecutive/Result clause. Indirect question.

5 The pupil was afraid that the teacher would ask why he had done this. (8 + 2)
Fear clause. Indirect question.

Total: 55

Exercise 22.11

1 Present.	volo.	6 Imperfect.	eo.
2 Imperfect.	volo.	7 Imperfect.	nolo.
3 Imperfect.	possum.	8 Imperfect.	video.
4 Imperfect.	sum.	9 Perfect.	amo.
5 Pluperfect.	sum.	10 Perfect.	deleo.

2 marks for each question. Total: 20

Exercise 22.12

1 Perfect.	incipio.	3 Imperfect.	debeo.
2 Pluperfect.	animadverto.	4 Present.	spero.

5	Imperfect.	nescio.	8	Imperfect.	puto.
6	Imperfect.	vereor.	9	Perfect.	progredior.
7	Present.	cognosco.	10	Present.	iuvo.

2 marks for each question. Total: 20

Exercise 22.13

1	Present.	amo.	6	Imperfect.	moneo.
2	Pluperfect.	rego.	7	Imperfect.	audio.
3	Perfect.	capio.	8	Imperfect.	sum.
4	Pluperfect.	video.	9	Perfect.	mitto.
5	Pluperfect.	dico.	10	Imperfect.	curro.

2 marks for each question. Total: 20

Exercise 22.14

1	Perfect.	persuadeo.	6	Perfect.	fero.
2	Pluperfect.	cogo.	7	Present.	custodio.
3	Imperfect.	fero.	8	Imperfect.	contendo.
4	Present.	pello.	9	Imperfect.	peto.
5	Imperfect.	interficio.	10	Perfect.	credo.

2 marks for each question. Total: 20

Exercise 22.15

1	Pluperfect.	convenio.	6	Imperfect.	effugio.
2	Perfect.	relinquo.	7	Present.	invenio.
3	Pluperfect.	occupo.	8	Perfect.	vinco.
4	Imperfect.	vulnero.	9	Present.	defendo.
5	Pluperfect.	occido.	10	Pluperfect.	conspicio.

2 marks for each question. Total: 20

Exercise 22.16

1 He is a boy, she is a girl, they are gods. (9)

2 The Romans often used to fight against the Greeks with swords and spears. (8)

3 The master punished the slave because he was bad. (6)

4 My house is bigger than yours. (6)

5 The water of that river is not clear. (6)

Total: 35

Exercise 23.1

The suitors were looking at the beggar in amazement.(4) He shouted:(1) 'I am Ulysses.(2) I have finally returned home.(3) Now I will punish you all.(4) Soon you will all be dead.'(4)

Having spoken these words he shot an arrow at Antinous.(5) Antinous fell to the ground dead.(4) There was uproar in the palace.(4) The suitors, having seen Antinous dead,(4) were afraid that they themselves would also soon be killed by Ulysses.(6) They were running about everywhere, looking for weapons.(4) There were none.(2) Meanwhile Ulysses and Telemachus were firing arrows at them.(6) They were so scared that they tried to escape from the palace.(6) In vain.(1) There was no escape.(3) Blood was flowing everywhere.(3) Soon piles of bodies were lying throughout the entire palace.(7) They had all been killed.(2)

Total: 75

Exercise 23.2

1 (a) petentes. (1)

   (b) conati sint. (1)

2 Subjunctive. (1)

3 Accusative. (1)

4 3rd.   Plural.   Pluperfect.   Indicative.   Passive.   **occido.**   (6)

Total: 10

Exercise 23.3

1 I ran quickly in order to escape.   (4 + 1)
   Final/Purpose clause.

2 I am asking you to stay.   (4 + 1)
   Indirect command.

3 He is so savage that no one likes him.   (7 + 1)
   Consecutive/Result clause.

4 While the boy was walking along the road he caught sight of a beautiful girl.   (8 + 1)
   cum-clause.

5 The teacher asked the boys not to play in the road.   (7 + 1)
   Indirect command.

6 When the soldiers had advanced they fought against the enemy. (7 + 1)
cum-clause.

7 We are going to the city to work. (5 + 1)
Final/Purpose clause.

8 Let us conquer the enemy, soldiers! (3 + 1)
Present independent subjunctive.

9 I am afraid that my father may punish me. (6 + 1)
Fear clause.

10 I did not know why the girls were running. (4 + 1)
Indirect question.

Total: 65

Exercise 23.4

1 The teacher ordered the pupils to work. (5 + 1)
Indirect command.

2 Let us stay here for a long time and drink wine, friends! (7 + 1)
Present independent subjunctive.

3 The master ordered the slave to carry the water home. (7 + 1)
Indirect command.

4 The soldier had received so many wounds that he soon died. (8 + 1)
Consecutive/Result clause.

5 The citizens fought bravely in order not to be captured by the enemy. (7 + 1)
Final/Purpose clause.

6 I do not know why that boy did this. (6 + 1)
Indirect question.

7 The storm is so savage that we are not able to sail out of harbour. (10 + 1)
Consecutive/Result clause.

8 I will persuade my wife to give me money. (7 + 1)
Indirect command.

9 Let us fight well, companions! (3 + 1)
Present independent subjunctive.

10 The teacher asked the boy what he wanted. (5 + 1)
Indirect question.

Total: 75

1 When the messenger had heard these words he departed. (6 + 1)
cum-clause.

2 Let us not be conquered! (2 + 1)
Present independent subjunctive.

3 The boy came home in order to sleep. (5 + 1)
Final/Purpose clause.

4 Teachers always order pupils to work. (6 + 1)
Indirect command.

5 I know what you (s.) are doing. (3 + 1)
Indirect question.

6 We were afraid that the enemy would arrive soon. (5 + 1)
Fear clause.

7 The boys are so tired that they are sleeping. (6 + 1)
Consecutive/Result clause.

8 Since the teacher was not wise, he did not know much. (8 + 1)
cum-clause.

9 I am working in order not to be punished. (3 + 1)
Final/Purpose clause.

10 Let me sleep! (1 + 1)
Present independent subjunctive.

Total: 55

1 I do not know why you (s.) did this. (4 + 1)
Indirect question.

2 This teacher is so cruel that he often punishes the pupils. (9 + 1)
Consecutive/Result clause.

3 Let us fight well, soldiers! (3 + 1)
Present independent subjunctive.

4 Who knows who he is? (4 + 1)
Indirect question.

5 There were so many enemy that we were afraid. (5 + 1)
Consecutive/Result clause.

6 We are working in order to become rich. (4 + 1)
Final/Purpose clause.

7 The girl was so afraid that she was crying. (5 + 1)
  Consecutive/Result clause.

8 I encouraged the boys to do this. (6 + 1)
  Indirect command.

9 Since the soldier had been wounded, he was not fighting well. (7 + 1)
  cum-clause.

10 We knew why they were running. (3 + 1)
   Indirect question.

Total: 60

Exercise 23.7

1 3rd person	Singular	Imperfect	Active	**possum**
2 3rd person	Singular	Pluperfect	Active	**volo**
3 3rd person	Singular	Perfect	Active	**incipio**
4 3rd person	Singular	Imperfect	Active	**narro**
5 3rd person	Plural	Present	Active	**sum**
6 3rd person	Singular	Imperfect	Deponent	**loquor**
7 3rd person	Plural	Present	Active	**eo**
8 3rd person	Singular	Perfect	Active	**deleo**
9 2nd person	Singular	Imperfect	Active	**video**
10 3rd person	Plural	Pluperfect	Active	**aedifico**

5 marks for each question. Total: 50

Exercise 23.8

1 This slave will be set free by his master tomorrow. (6)

2 Teachers often say many words. (5)

3 The girl shows/showed the gift to her friends. (4)

4 Why does no one believe me? (4)

5 I have never seen a more beautiful girl than that one. (6)

Total: 25

Exercise 24.1

There was silence.(2) Penelope looked at the bodies of the suitors, then at Ulysses.(5) He was looking at her.(2) Finally he said: 'I am Ulysses, king of Ithaca, your husband.'(8) Penelope remained motionless.(3) She did not know whether this man was really Ulysses or not.(6) She therefore decided to test him.(4) She shouted:(1) 'Maidservant, this man is so tired that he wants to sleep.(9) Bring my bed here!'(4) When he heard this, Ulysses was so angry that he shouted:(7) 'My bed hasn't been broken, has it, Penelope?(4) I made the bed myself.(3) Part of the bed is a tree.(4) It cannot be moved.'(3) When Penelope heard these words she immediately knew that this man was really Ulysses.(10) She ran to him and embraced him.(5) Both Ulysses and Penelope were so happy that they began to cry.(9) After so many years they were finally together.(6)

Total: 95

Exercise 24.2

1 (a) ille/hic/hoc/haec/hunc.   (1)

  (b) velit.   (1)

2 Subjunctive.   Consecutive clause.   (2)

3 Accusative.   Object of the verb.   (2)

4 Perfect.   Subjunctive.   Active.   incipio.   (4)

Total: 10

Exercise 24.3

1 This soldier was wounded to such an extent that he was not able to fight.   (9 + 1)
  Consecutive/Result clause.

2 When the boys saw this, they laughed.   (5 + 1)
  ut + indicative.

3 The woman ordered her daughter to run.   (5 + 1)
  Indirect command.

4 This soldier fights so well that he is never wounded by the enemy.   (10 + 1)
  Consecutive/Result clause.

5 The beggar used to ask the suitors to give food to him.   (7 + 1)
  Indirect command.

6 These pupils, as you see, are not wise. (7 + 1)
  ut + indicative.

7 The boy is coming/has come home to sleep. (5 + 1)
  Final/Purpose clause.

8 This master was so rich that he had many slaves. (9 + 1)
  Consecutive/Result clause.

9 The soldiers fought bravely in order not to be conquered by the enemy. (7 + 1)
  Final/Purpose clause.

10 The wise master ordered the slave not to play. (6 + 1)
  Indirect command.

Total: 80

Exercise 24.4

1 The general ordered this soldier to fight well. (7)

2 I was able to see what he had done. (5)

3 I will persuade my friend to write a book. (6)

4 I persuaded my friend to write a book. (6)

5 The women were afraid that they would be captured by the enemy within a few days. (8)

6 That old man was so tired that he was not able to walk. (9)

7 The Romans, as you know, were very good soldiers. (6)

8 The soldier received so many wounds that he fell to the ground. (8)

9 The general wanted to find out where the forces of the enemy were. (7)

10 The girl was so sad that she suddenly began to cry. (8)

Total: 70

Exercise 24.5

1 There was such a great uproar in the palace that the suitors were running everywhere. (9)

2 We all know that the Romans are the best soldiers. (6)

3 The suitors did not know whether they were able to escape or not. (6)

4 Ulysses knew that his bed could not be moved. (7)

5 Since I am poor, I do not have much money. (7)

6 Ulysses had built the bed in such a way that it could not be moved. (8)

7 I hope that I will see that girl tomorrow. (7)

8 Ulysses announced that he would kill all the suitors. (7)

9 Penelope did not believe that this man was Ulysses. (7)

10 I saw many girls lying on the beach. (6)

Total: 70

Exercise 24.6

1 The suitors knew that they could not escape. (6)

2 The suitors knew that they would be killed by Ulysses. (7)

3 Penelope ordered the maidservant to move the bed. (6)

4 Penelope said this in order to test Ulysses. (6)

5 The Greeks hid many soldiers in the huge horse in order to capture the city of Troy. (11)

6 Ulysses looked at the suitors running everywhere. (5)

7 The Trojans were so amazed that they did not know what they ought to do. (9)

8 The storm was so great that the ships were not able to set out from the harbour. (10)

9 This teacher is always encouraging his pupils to read books. (8)

10 Good pupils read books in order to become wise. (7)

Total: 75

Exercise 24.7

1 The old man did not know who had built the temple. (5 + 1)
Indirect question.

2 I do not know whether I have read this book or not. (6 + 1)
Indirect question.

3 The general was so brave that everyone used to praise him. (8 + 1)
Consecutive/Result clause.

4 The wives will ask their husbands to give them money. (7 + 1)
Indirect command.

5 The general was afraid that the soldiers had been captured. (6 + 1)
Fear clause.

6 The father asked his son to make the journey with him. (7 + 1)
Indirect command.

7 The master asked himself what he ought to do. (6 + 1)
Indirect question.

8 I am warning you not to drink this water. (6 + 1)
Indirect command.

9 The small boy asked everyone whether they had seen his parents. (7 + 1)
Indirect question.

10 The general of the enemy was so afraid that he fled immediately. (7 + 1)
Consecutive/Result clause.

Total: 75

Exercise 24.8

1 He asked the soldiers why they had fought against the Romans for so many years. (8 + 1)
Indirect question.

2 The Greeks believed that they would never be conquered by the Romans. (8 + 1)
Indirect statement.

3 The Greeks knew that they were not able to fight for a long time. (7 + 1)
Indirect statement.

4 The Romans advanced in order to charge at the enemy. (7 + 1)
Final/Purpose clause.

5 The mother asked her husband not to punish their bad son. (7 + 1)
Indirect command.

6 He himself says that he is wise. (5 + 1)
Indirect statement.

7 Caesar ordered the soldiers to pitch camp. (6 + 1)
Indirect command.

8 I am asking you to stay here. (5 + 1)
Indirect command.

9 This boy is so stupid that he knows nothing. (8 + 1)
Consecutive/Result clause.

10 Tell me who you (s.) are! (4 + 1)
Indirect question.

Total: 75

Exercise 24.9

1 The boy said to this father that he was frightened that he would be punished by the teacher.
Indirect statement. Fear clause.

2 The general said that he would order the soldiers to attack the town.
Indirect statement. Indirect command.

3 The master entered the villa in order to see whether the slaves were working or not.
Final/Purpose clause. Indirect question.

4 All the pupils were afraid that the teacher would ask why they were not working.
   Fear clause. Indirect question.

5 The messenger ran quickly in order to announce to the general that the enemy had been conquered.
   Final/Purpose clause. Indirect statement.

9 + 2 marks for each question. Total: 55

Exercise 24.10

1 3rd person	Singular	Perfect	Active	dico
2 3rd person	Singular	Imperfect	Active	pono
3 3rd person	Singular	Present	Active	eo
4 1st person	Plural	Pluperfect	Active	maneo
5 3rd person	Plural	Imperfect	Passive	conspicio
6 3rd person	Plural	Perfect	Active	do
7 3rd person	Plural	Imperfect	Passive	paro
8 3rd person	Singular	Imperfect	Active	sto
9 1st person	Plural	Present	Passive	laudo
10 2nd person	Singular	Pluperfect	Active	mitto

5 marks for each question. Total: 50

Exercise 24.11

1 The ships set out from the harbour at first light. (7)

2 Poor men do not have much money. (6)

3 Many gifts used to be given to the soldiers by the general. (6)

4 No one however will be able to do this. (5)

5 The daughter of the teacher is preparing a very good dinner for her father. (6)

Total: 30